Logic Primer

Logic Primer

Colin Allen and Michael Hand

A Bradford Book

The MIT Press
Cambridge, Massachusetts
London, England

Printed and bound in the United States of America.

Library of Congress Cataloging-in-Publication Data

Allen, Colin.
Logic primer/Colin Allen and Michael Hand.—2nd ed.
p. cm.
"A Bradford book."
Includes bibliographical references and index.
ISBN 0-262-51126-6 (pbk.: alk. paper)
1. Logic. I. Hand, Michael. II. Title

BC108.A543 2001
160—dc21

00-048960

10 9 8 7 6 5 4 3 2

to Lynn and Susan

Contents

Preface

To the Student

The most important thing for you to know about this book is that it is designed to be used with a teacher. You should not expect to learn logic from this book alone (although it will be possible if you have had experience with formal systems or can make use of the website at http://mitpress.mit.edu/LogicPrimer/). We have deliberately reduced to a minimum the amount of explanatory material, relying upon your instructor to expand on the ideas. Our goal has been to produce a text in which all of the material is important, thus saving you the expense of a yellow marker pen. Consequently, you should never turn a page of this book until you understand it thoroughly.

The text consists of *Definitions*, Examples, *Comments*, and Exercises. (Exercises marked with asterisks are answered at the back of the book.) The comments are of two sorts. Those set in full-size type contain material we deem essential to the text. Those set in smaller type are relatively incidental—the ideas they contain are not essential to the flow of the book, but they provide perspective on the two logical systems you will learn.

In this age of large classes and diminished personal contact between students and their teachers, we hope this book promotes a rewarding learning experience.

To the Teacher

We wrote this book because we were dissatisfied with the logic texts now available. The authors of those texts talk too much. Students neither need nor want page after page of explanation that require them to turn back and forth among statements of rules, examples, and discussion. They prefer having their teachers explain things to them—after all, students take notes. Consequently, one of our goals has been to produce a text of minimal chattiness, leaving to the instructor the task of providing explanations. Only an instructor in a given classroom can be expected to know how best to explain the material to the students in that class, and we choose not to force upon the instructor any particular mode of explanation.

Another reason our for dissatisfaction was that most texts contain material that we are not interested in teaching in an introductory logic class. Some logic texts, and indeed some very popular ones, contain chapters on informal fallacies, theories of definition, or inductive logic, and some contain more than one deductive apparatus. Consequently, we found ourselves ordering texts for a single-semester course and covering no more than half of the material in them. This book is intended for a one-semester course in which propositional logic and predicate logic are introduced, but no metatheory. (Any student who has mastered the material in this book will be well prepared to take a second course on metatheory, using Lemmon's classic, *Beginning Logic*, or even Tennant's *Natural Logic*.)

We prefer systems of natural deduction to other ways of representing arguments, and we have adopted Lemmon's technique of explicitly tracking assumptions on each line of a proof. We find that this technique illuminates the relation between conclusions and premises better than other devices for managing assumptions. Besides that, it allows for shorter, more elegant proofs. A given assumption can be discharged more than once, so that it need not be assumed again in order to be discharged again. Thus, the following is possible, and there is no need to assume P twice:

1	(1)	$P \rightarrow (Q \& R)$	assume
2	(2)	P	assume
1,2	(3)	Q & R	from 1,2

1,2	(4)	Q	from 3
1,2	(5)	R	from 3
1	(6)	P → Q	from 4, discharge 2
1	(7)	P → R	from 5, discharge 2
1	(8)	(P → Q) & (P → R)	from 6,7

Clearly, the notion of subderivation has no application in such a system. The alternative approach involving subderivations allows a given assumption to be discharged only once, so the following is needed:

(1)	P → (Q & R)	assume
(2)	P	assume
(3)	Q & R	from 1,2
(4)	Q	from 3
(5)	P → Q	from 4, discharge 2
(6)	P	assume
(7)	Q & R	from 1,6 (same inference as at 3!)
(8)	R	from 7
(9)	P → R	from 8, discharge 6
(10)	(P → Q) & (P → R)	from 5,9

The redundancy of this proof is obvious. Nonetheless, an instructor who prefers subderivation-style proofs can use our system by changing the rules concerning assumption sets as follows: (i) Every line has the assumption set of the immediately preceding line, except when an assumption is discharged. (ii) The only assumption available for discharge at a given line is the highest-numbered assumption in the assumption set. (iii) After an assumption has been discharged, that line number can never again appear in a later assumption set. (In other words, the assumption-set device becomes a stack or a first-in-last-out memory device.)

There are a number of other differences between our system and Lemmon's, including a different set of primitive rules of proof. What follows is a listing of the more significant differences between our system and Lemmon's, together with reasons we prefer our system.

- Lemmon disallows vacuous discharge of assumptions. We allow it. Thus it is correct in our system to discharge an assumption by reductio ad absurdum when the contradiction does not depend on that assumption. Whenever vacuous discharge occurs, one can obtain a Lemmon-acceptable deduction by means of trivial additions to the proof. We prefer to avoid these additions. (Note that Lemmon's preclusion of vacuous discharge means that accomplishing the same effect requires redundant steps of &-introduction and &-elimination. For instance, Lemmon requires (a) to prove $P \vdash Q \rightarrow P$, while we allow (b).

(a)

1	(1)	P	assume
2	(2)	Q	assume
1,2	(3)	Q & P	from 1,2
1,2	(4)	P	from 3
1	(5)	Q $\rightarrow$ P	from 4, discharge 2

(b)

1	(1)	P	assume
2	(2)	Q	assume
1	(3)	Q $\rightarrow$ P	from 1, discharge 2

- Lemmon's characterization of proof entails that an argument has been established as valid only when a proof has been given in which the conclusion depends on all of the argument's premises. This is needlessly restrictive, since in some valid arguments the conclusion is in fact provable from a proper subset of the premises. We remove this restriction, allowing a proof for a given argument to rest its conclusion on some but not all of the argument's premises.

- We have replaced Lemmon's primitive ∨-Elimination rule by what is normally known as Disjunctive Syllogism (DS). We realize that Lemmon's rule is philosophically preferable, as it is a pure rule; however, DS is so much easier to learn that pedagogical considerations outweigh philosophical ones in this case.

- Despite the preceding point, we have kept the ∃-elimination rule used by Lemmon. Although slightly more complicated than the more common rule of ∃−Instantiation, this rule frees the student from having to remember to instantiate existential quantifications before instantiating universal quantifications. It also frees the student from having to examine the not-yet-reached conclusion of the argument, to determine which instantial names are unavailable for a given application of ∃-Instantiation. Furthermore, at any point in a proof using ∃-elimination, some argument has been proven. If the proof has reached a line of the form

    m,...,n   (k)   z   ...

then the sentence z has been established as provable from the premise set {m,...,n}. (Here the right-hand ellipsis indicates which rule was applied to yield z, and which earlier sentences it was applied to.) This is quite useful in helping the student understand what is going on in a proof. In a system using ∃-instantiation, however, this feature is absent: there are correct proofs some of whose lines do not follow from previous lines, since the rule of ∃-instantiation is not a valid rule. For instance, the following is the beginning of a proof using ∃-instantiation.

| 1 | (1) | ∃xFx | assumption |
| 1 | (2) | Fa | 1 ∃-instantiation |

Line 2 does not follow from line 1. This difference between ∃-elimination and ∃-instantiation can be put as follows: in an ∃-elimination proof, you can stop at any time and still have a correct proof of some argument or other, but in an ∃-instantiation proof, you cannot stop whenever you like. It seems to us that these implications of ∃-instantiation's invalidity outweigh the additional complexity of ∃-elimination. In an ∃-elimination system, not only is the *system* sound as a whole, but every rule is individually valid; this is not true for an ∃-instantiation system.

•   Whereas Lemmon requires that existentialization (existential generalization) replace all tokens of the generalized name by tokens of the bound variable, we allow existentialization to pick up only some of the tokens of the generalized name.

•   We have abandoned Lemmon's distinction between proper names and arbitrary names, which is not essential in a natural deduction system. The conditions on quantifier rules ensure that the instantial name is arbitrary in the appropriate sense. (We comment on this motivation for the conditions in the text.)

In many cases, we have deliberately not used quotation marks to indicate that an expression of the formal language is being mentioned. In general, we use single quotes to indicate mention only when confusion might result. (We hope no one is antagonized by this flaunting of convention. Trained philosophers may at first find the absence of quotes disconcerting, but we believe that we are making things easier without leading the student astray significantly.)

We have tried to present the material in a way that reveals clearly the systematic organization of the text. This manner of presentation makes it especially easy for students to review the material when studying, and to look up particular points when the need arises. Consequently, there is little discursive prose in the text, and what seemed unavoidable has been relegated to the *Comments*. We hope to have produced a small text that is truly student-oriented but that still allows the instructor a maximum of flexibility in presenting the material.

The Second Edition
With one exception, the changes to the second edition have been minimal. We have added a treatment of identity to chapters 3 and 4. In chapter 3 this required merely a slight modification to the definition of wff, some comments on translation, and the inclusion of introduction and elimination rules for identity. The changes made to chapter 4 are more extensive. In the first edition we avoided overt reference to the object language/metalanguage distinction and had no need to introduce into the specification of interpretations the extensions (denotations, referents) of names, but the inclusion of identity in the language necessitates them. To keep matters simple, when giving interpretations for sentences that involve identity we use italicized names in the metalanguage, and we recommend that no member of the universe of an interpretation be given more than one metalinguistic name. This makes it easy to specify whether or not two names of the object

language have the same extension in an interpretation, for the same metalinguistic name will be used for names denoting the same object. Expansions now involve the use of italicized names, so that strictly speaking they are not wffs of the object language. This does not affect their use in determining truth values of quantified wffs in an interpretation, and facilitates their use in determining truth values of wffs involving identity. (We realize that italicization is not available for hand-written exercises, so we recommend that instructors adopt a convention such as underlining for blackboard presentations.) The addition of the material on identity is supplemented with new exercises in chapters 3 and 4. We have tried to organize the new material in such a way that an instructor who wishes to omit it can do so easily.

In chapter 1, a set of exercises has been inserted whose proofs do not require →I and RAA. That is, these proofs do not involve the discharge of assumptions. These exercises are intended to allow students to become comfortable with the remaining rules of proof before they are forced to learn the more complicated mechanics of →I and RAA.

In chapter 3 we have waited until after the section on translations to introduce the notions of a wff's universalization, existentialization, and instance. This change reduces the chance of the student's confusing the rules for constructing universally quantified wffs, where at least one occurrence of a name must be replaced by a variable, and universalization, where all occurrences of the name must be replaced.

Web Support

A variety of interactive exercises and an automated proof checker for the proof systems introduced in this book can be accessed at http://mitpress.mit.edu/LogicPrimer/. Use of the software requires nothing more than a basic web browser running on any kind of computer.

Acknowledgements

We were unfortunately remiss in the first edition in failing to thank Harry Stanton for his encouragement to write this text. We gratefully acknowledge the comments we have received from colleagues who have taught from the first edition, particularly Jon Kvanvig and Chris Menzel. A number of typographical errors were identified by an extremely meticulous self-study reader from the Midwest whose identity has become lost to us and whom we encourage to contact us again (and to accept our apologies). Chris Menzel also receives credit for his extensive (and voluntary) work on the web software. Finally, Amy Kind deserves special thanks for her help with the website and for her most useful comments on the manuscript for the second edition.

Logic Primer

Chapter 1
Sentential Logic

1.1 **Basic logical notions**

argument,
premises,
conclusion

Definition. An **ARGUMENT** is a pair of things:
- a set of sentences, the **PREMISES**
- a sentence, the **CONCLUSION**.

Comment. All arguments have conclusions, but not all arguments have premises: the set of premises can be the empty set! Later we shall examine this idea in some detail.

Comment. If the sentences involved belong to English (or any other natural language), we need to specify that the premises and the conclusion are sentences that can be true or false. That is, the premises and the conclusion must all be declarative (or indicative) sentences such as 'The cat is on the mat' or 'I am here', and not sentences such as 'Is the cat on the mat?' (interrogative) or 'Come here!' (imperative). We are going to construct some formal languages in which every sentence is either true or false. Thus this qualification is not present in the definition above.

validity

Definition. An argument is **VALID** if and only if it is necessary that *if* all its premises are true, its conclusion is true.

Comment. The intuitive idea captured by this definition is this: If it is possible for the conclusion of an argument to be false when its premises are all true, then the argument is not reliable (that is, it is invalid).

If true premises guarantee a true conclusion then the argument is valid.

Alternate formulation of the definition. An argument is **VALID** if and only if it is impossible for all the premises to be true while the conclusion is false.

entailment   *Definition.* When an argument is valid we say that its premises **ENTAIL** its conclusion.

soundness   *Definition.* An argument is **SOUND** if and only if it is valid and all its premises are true.

Comment. It follows that all sound arguments have true conclusions.

Comment. An argument may be unsound in either of two ways: it is invalid, or it has one or more false premises.

Comment. The rest of this book is concerned with validity rather than soundness.

Exercise 1.1   Indicate whether each of the following sentences is True or False.

i*   Every premise of a valid argument is true.
ii*   Every invalid argument has a false conclusion.
iii*   Every valid argument has exactly two premises.
iv*   Some valid arguments have false conclusions.
v*   Some valid arguments have a false conclusion despite having premises that are all true.

vi*	A sound argument cannot have a false conclusion.
vii*	Some sound arguments are invalid.
viii*	Some unsound arguments have true premises.
ix*	Premises of sound arguments entail their conclusions.
x*	If an argument has true premises and a true conclusion then it is sound.

1.2   **A Formal Language for Sentential Logic**

formal   *Comment.* To represent similarities among arguments
language   of a natural language, logicians introduce formal
                      languages. The first formal language we will introduce
                      is the language of sentential logic (also known as
                      propositional logic). In chapter 3 we introduce a more
                      sophisticated language: that of predicate logic.

vocabulary   *Definition.* The **VOCABULARY OF SENTENTIAL
                      LOGIC** consists of
                      • **SENTENCE LETTERS,**
                      • **CONNECTIVES**, and
                      • **PARENTHESES.**

sentence   *Definition.* A **SENTENCE LETTER** is any symbol
letter   from the following list:
$$A, \ldots, Z, A_0, \ldots, Z_0, A_1, \ldots, Z_1, \ldots.$$

sentence   *Comment.* By the use of subscripts we make available
variable   an infinite number of sentence letters. These sentence
                      letters are also sometimes called **SENTENCE VARI-
                      ABLES**, because we use them to stand for sentences
                      of natural languages.

connectives   *Definition.* The **SENTENTIAL CONNECTIVES** (often just called **CONNECTIVES**) are the members of the following list: ~, &, ∨, →, ↔.

Comment. The sentential connectives correspond to various words in natural languages that serve to connect declarative sentences.

tilde   ~   The **TILDE** corresponds to the English 'It is not the case that'. (In this case the use of the term 'connective' is odd, since only one declarative sentence is negated at a time.)

ampersand &   The **AMPERSAND** corresponds to the English 'Both … and …'.

wedge   ∨   The **WEDGE** corresponds to the English 'Either … or …' in its inclusive sense.

arrow   →   The **ARROW** corresponds to the English 'If … then …'.

**double-
arrow**   ↔   The **DOUBLE-ARROW** corresponds to the English 'if and only if'.

Comment. Natural languages typically provide more than one way to express a given connection between sentences. For instance, the sentence 'John is dancing but Mary is sitting down' expresses the same logical relationship as 'John is dancing and Mary is sitting down'. The issue of translation from English to the formal language is taken up in section 1.3.

) and (The right and left parentheses are used as punctuation marks for the language.

expression   *Definition.* An **EXPRESSION** of sentential logic is any sequence of sentence letters, sentential connectives, or left and right parentheses.

Examples.
(P → Q) is an expression of sentential logic.
)PQ→~ is also an expression of sentential logic.
(3 → 4) is not an expression of sentential logic.

metavariable   *Definition.* Greek letters such as ϕ and ψ are used as **METAVARIABLES.** They are not themselves parts of the language of sentential logic, but they stand for expressions of the language.

Comment. (ϕ → ψ) is not an expression of sentential logic, but it may be used to represent an expression of sentential logic.

well-formed   *Definition.* A **WELL-FORMED FORMULA** (**WFF**)
formula   of sentential logic is any expression that accords with
the following seven rules:

(1) **A sentence letter standing alone is a wff.**

atomic   [*Definition.* The sentence letters are the **ATOMIC**
sentence   **SENTENCES** of the language of sentential logic.]

(2) **If φ is a wff, then the expression denoted by ~φ is also a wff.**

negation   [*Definition.* A wff of this form is known as a **NEGA-TION**, and ~φ is known as the **NEGATION OF** φ.]

(3) **If φ and ψ are both wffs, then the expression denoted by (φ & ψ) is a wff.**

conjunction   [*Definition.* A wff of this form is known as a **CON-JUNCTION**. φ and ψ are known as the left and right **CONJUNCTS**, respectively.]

(4) **If φ and ψ are both wffs, then the expression denoted by (φ ∨ ψ) is a wff.**

disjunction   [*Definition.* A wff of this form is known as a **DIS-JUNCTION**. φ and ψ are the left and right **DISJUNCTS**, respectively.]

(5) **If φ and ψ are both wffs, then the expression denoted by (φ → ψ) is a wff.**

conditional,
antecedent,
consequent

[*Definition.* A wff of this form is known as a **CONDI-TIONAL.** The wff ϕ is known as the **ANTECEDENT** of the conditional. The wff ψ is known as the **CONSEQUENT** of the conditional.]

(6) **If ϕ and ψ are both wffs, then the expression denoted by (ϕ ↔ ψ) is a wff.**

biconditional

[*Definition.* A wff of this form is known as a **BICONDITIONAL.** It is also sometimes known as an **EQUIVALENCE.**]

(7) **Nothing else is a wff.**

binary
and unary
connectives

Definition. &, ∨, →, and ↔ are **BINARY CONNEC-TIVES,** since they connect two wffs together. ~ is a **UNARY CONNECTIVE,** since it attaches to a single wff.

sentence

Definition. A **SENTENCE** of the formal language is a wff that is not part of a larger wff.

denial

Definition. The **DENIAL** of a wff ϕ that is not a negation is ~ϕ. A negation, ~ϕ, has two **DENIALS:** ϕ and ~~ϕ.

Example.
~(P → Q) has one negation: ~~(P → Q)
It has two denials: (P → Q) and ~~(P → Q).

(P → Q) has just one denial: its negation, ~(P → Q).

Comment. The reason for introducing the ideas of a sentence and a denial will be apparent when the rules of proof are introduced in section 1.4.

Exercise 1.2.1 Which of the following expressions are wffs? If an expression is a wff, say whether it is an atomic sentence, a conditional, a conjunction, a disjunction, a negation, or a biconditional. For the binary connectives, identify the component wffs (antecedent, consequent, conjuncts, disjuncts, etc.).

i*	A
ii*	(A
iii*	(A)
iv*	(A → B)
v*	(A → (
vi*	(A → (B → C))
vii*	((P & Q) → R)
viii*	((A & B) ∨ (C → (D ↔ G)))
ix*	~(A → B)
x*	~(P → Q) ∨ ~(Q & R)
xi*	~(A)
xii*	(~A) → B
xiii*	(~(P & P) & (P ↔ (Q ∨ ~Q)))
xiv*	(~((B ∨ P) & C) ↔ ((D ∨ ~G) → H))
xv*	(~(Q ∨ ~(B)) ∨ (E ↔ (D ∨ X)))

parenthesis-dropping conventions

Comment. For ease of reading, it is often convenient to drop parentheses from wffs, so long as no ambiguity results. If a sentence is surrounded by parentheses then these may be dropped.

Example.
P → Q will be read as shorthand for (P → Q).

Comment. Where parentheses are embedded within sentences we must be careful if we are to omit any parentheses. For example, the expression P & Q → R is potentially ambiguous between ((P & Q) → R) and (P & (Q → R)). To resolve such ambiguities, we adopt the following convention: ~ binds more strongly than all the other connectives; & and ∨ bind component expressions more strongly than →, which in turn binds its components more strongly than ↔.

Examples.
~P & Q → R is read as ((~P & Q) → R).
P → Q ↔ R is read as ((P → Q) ↔ R).
P ∨ Q & R is not allowed, as it is ambiguous between
        (P ∨ (Q & R)) and ((P ∨ Q) & R).
P → Q → R is not allowed, as it is ambiguous between
        (P → (Q → R)) and ((P → Q) → R).

Comment. The expressions admitted by these parenthesis-dropping conventions are not themselves well-formed formulas of sentential logic.

Exercise 1.2.2 Rewrite all the sentences in exercise 1.2.1 above, using the parenthesis-dropping conventions. Omit any parentheses you can without introducing ambiguity.

Exercise 1.2.3 State whether each of the following is ambiguous or unambiguous, given the parenthesis-dropping conventions. In the unambiguous cases, write out the sentences and reinstate all omitted parentheses.

i*	$P \leftrightarrow \sim Q \vee R$
ii*	$P \vee Q \to R \,\&\, S$
iii*	$P \vee Q \to R \leftrightarrow S$
iv*	$P \vee Q \,\&\, R \to \sim S$
v*	$P \to R \,\&\, S \to T$
vi*	$P \to Q \to R \to S$
vii*	$P \,\&\, Q \leftrightarrow \sim R \vee S$
viii*	$\sim P \,\&\, Q \vee R \to S \leftrightarrow T$
ix*	$P \to Q \,\&\, \sim R \leftrightarrow \sim S \vee T \to U$
x*	$P \to Q \,\&\, \sim R \to \sim S \vee T \leftrightarrow U$

1.3   **Translation of English to Sentential Wffs**

translation scheme

Definition. A **TRANSLATION SCHEME** for the language of sentential logic is a pairing of sentence letters with sentences of a natural language. The sentences in a translation scheme should be logically simple. That is, they should not contain any of the words corresponding to the sentential connectives.

logical form   *Definition.* The **LOGICAL FORM** of a sentence of a natural language relative to a translation scheme is given by its translation into a wff of sentential logic according to that translation scheme.

Example.
Under the translation scheme
  P: John does well at logic
  Q: Bill is happy
The sentence
  If John does well at logic, then Bill is happy
has the logical form $(P \to Q)$.

Comment. English provides many different ways of stating negations, conditionals, conjunctions, disjunctions, and biconditionals. Thus, many different sentences of English may have the same logical form.

stylistic   *Definition.* If two sentences of a natural language have
variants   the same logical form relative to a single translation scheme, they are said to be **STYLISTIC VARIANTS** of each other.

Comment. There are far too many stylistic variants of negations, conjunctions, disjunctions, conjunctions, and biconditionals to list here. The follow is a partial list of stylistic variants in each category.

negations   Let P translate the sentence 'John is conscious.' Here
are a few of the ways of expressing ~P:
   John is not conscious.
   John is unconscious.
   It is not the case that John is conscious.
   It is false that John is conscious.

conditionals   Stylistic variants whose logical form is $(\phi \rightarrow \psi)$,
where ϕ is the antecedent and ψ is the consequent
include the following:
   If ϕ, ψ.
   ϕ only if ψ.
   ϕ is a sufficient condition for ψ.
   ϕ is sufficient for ψ.
   Provided that ϕ, ψ.
   ψ provided that ϕ.
   ψ on the condition that ϕ.
   ψ is a necessary condition for ϕ.
   ψ is necessary for ϕ.
   Whenever ϕ, ψ.
   ψ if ϕ.
   Given that ϕ, ψ.
   In case ϕ, ψ.
   ϕ only on the condition that ψ.

conjunctions   Variants with logical form (ϕ & ψ) include the following:

> ϕ and ψ.
>
> Both ϕ and ψ.
>
> ϕ, but ψ.
>
> ϕ, although ψ.
>
> ϕ as well as ψ.
>
> Though ϕ, ψ.
>
> ϕ, also ψ.

disjunctions   Variants with logical form ($\phi \vee \psi$) include these:

> ϕ or ψ.
>
> Either ϕ or ψ.
>
> ϕ unless ψ.

Comment. 'ϕ unless ψ' is also commonly translated as ($\sim\psi \rightarrow \phi$). The proof techniques introduced in section 1.4 can be used to show that this is equivalent to ($\phi \vee \psi$).

biconditionals Variants having the logical form ($\phi \leftrightarrow \psi$) include the following:

> ϕ if and only if ψ.
>
> ϕ is equivalent to ψ.
>
> ϕ is necessary and sufficient for ψ.
>
> ϕ just in case ψ.

neither...   English sentences of the form 'Neither ϕ nor ψ' have
nor ...   the logical form $\sim(\phi \vee \psi)$, or, equivalently, ($\sim\phi$ & $\sim\psi$).

tenses   *Comment.* In English, the sentences 'Mary is dancing' and 'Mary will dance' have different meanings because of the tenses of their respective verbs. In some cases, when one is analyzing arguments it is important to preserve the distinction between tenses. In other cases, the distinction can be ignored. In general, a judgment call is required to decide whether or not tense can be safely ignored.

Example.
Consider the following two arguments:

A   If Mary is dancing, John will dance.
    Mary is dancing.
    Therefore, John is dancing.

B   If Mary dances, John will dance.
    If John dances, Bill will dance.
    Therefore, if Mary dances, Bill will dance.

In A, if the difference between 'John will dance' and 'John is dancing' is ignored, then the argument will look valid in translation. But this seems unreasonable on inspection of the English.

In B, ignoring the difference between 'John will dance' and 'John dances' also makes the argument valid in translation. In this case, however, this seems reasonable.

In the translation exercises that follow, assume that tense distinctions may be ignored.

Exercise 1.3   Translate the following sentences into the language of sentential logic.

Translation scheme for 1–20
P: John dances.
Q: Mary dances.
R: Bill dances.
S: John is happy.
T: Mary is happy.
U: Bill is happy.

1*	John is dancing but Mary is not dancing.
2*	If John does not dance, then Mary will not be happy.
3*	John's dancing is sufficient to make Mary happy.
4*	John's dancing is necessary to make Mary happy.
5*	John will not dance unless Mary is happy.
6*	If John's dancing is necessary for Mary to be happy, Bill will be unhappy.
7*	If Mary dances although John is not happy, Bill will dance.
8*	If neither John nor Bill is dancing, Mary is not happy.
9*	Mary is not happy unless either John or Bill is dancing.
10*	Mary will be happy if both John and Bill dance.
11*	Although neither John nor Bill is dancing, Mary is happy.
12*	If Bill dances, then if Mary dances John will too.
13*	Mary will be happy only if Bill is happy.

14*   Neither John nor Bill will dance if Mary is not happy.

15*   If Mary dances only if Bill dances and John dances
             only if Mary dances, then John dances only if Bill
             dances.

16*   Mary will dance if John or Bill but not both dance.

17*   If John dances and so does Mary, but Bill does not,
             then Mary will not be happy but John and Bill will.

18*   Mary will be happy if and only if John is happy.

19*   Provided that Bill is unhappy, John will not dance
             unless Mary is dancing.

20*   If John dances on the condition that if he dances Mary
             dances, then he dances.

             Translation scheme for 21–25
             P: A purpose of punishment is deterrence.
             Q: Capital punishment is an effective deterrent.
             R: Capital punishment should be continued.
             S: Capital punishment is used in the United States.
             T: A purpose of punishment is retribution.

21*   If a purpose of punishment is deterrence and capital
             punishment is an effective deterrent, then capital pun-
             ishment should be continued.

22*   Capital punishment is not an effective deterrent al-
             though it is used in the United States.

23*   Capital punishment should not be continued if it is not
             an effective deterrent, unless deterrence is not a pur-
             pose of punishment.

24*   If retribution is a purpose of punishment but deterrence
             is not, then capital punishment should not be con-
             tinued.

25*   Capital punishment should be continued even though
             capital punishment is not an effective deterrent pro-
             vided that a purpose of punishment is retribution in
             addition to deterrence.

1.4   Primitive Rules of Proof

turnstile   *Definition.* The **TURNSTILE** is the symbol ⊢.

sequent   *Definition.* A **SEQUENT** consists of a number of
                    sentences separated by commas (corresponding to the
                    premises of an argument), followed by a turnstile,
                    followed by another sentence (corresponding to the
                    conclusion of the argument).
                    Example. $(P \& Q) \rightarrow R, \sim R \& P \vdash \sim Q$

                    Comment. Sequents are nothing more than a
                    convenient way of displaying arguments in the formal
                    notation. The turnstile symbol may be read as
                    'therefore'.

proof   *Definition.* A **PROOF** is a sequence of lines contain-
                    ing sentences. Each sentence is either an assumption or
                    the result of applying a rule of proof to earlier
                    sentences in the sequence. The primitive rules of proof
                    are stated below.

Comment. The purpose of presenting proofs is to demonstrate *unequivocally* that a given set of premises entails a particular conclusion. Thus, when presenting a proof we associate three things with each sentence in the proof sequence:

annotation   On the right of the sentence we provide an **ANNOTATION** specifying which rule of proof was applied to which earlier sentences to yield the given sentence.

assumption set On the far left we associate with each sentence an **ASSUMPTION SET** containing the assumptions on which the given sentence depends.

line number   Also on the left, we write the current **LINE NUMBER** of the proof.

line of proof *Definition.* A sentence of a proof, together with its annotation, its assumption set and the line number, is called a **LINE OF THE PROOF**.

Example.

$$1,2 \quad (7) \quad P \rightarrow Q \,\&\, R \qquad\qquad 6 \rightarrow I\ (3)$$

$\uparrow$ Line number $\uparrow$ Annotation

Assumption set   Sentence

proof for   *Definition.* A **PROOF FOR A GIVEN ARGUMENT**
a given   is a proof whose last sentence is the argument's
argument   conclusion depending on nothing other than the argument's premises.

**primitive
rules**

Definition. The ten **PRIMITIVE RULES OF PROOF** are the rules assumption, ampersand-introduction, ampersand-elimination, wedge-introduction, wedge-elimination, arrow-introduction, arrow-elimination, reductio ad absurdum, double-arrow-introduction, and double-arrow-elimination, as described below.

assumption

Assume any sentence.

Annotation:	**A**
Assumption set:	The current line number.
Comment:	Anything may be assumed at any time. However, some assumptions are useful and some are not!

Example.

1   (1)   P ∨ Q   A

**ampersand-
intro**

Given two sentences (at lines *m* and *n*), conclude a conjunction of them.

Annotation:	***m, n*** &I
Assumption set:	The union of the assumption sets at lines *m* and *n*.
Comment:	The order of lines *m* and *n* in the proof is irrelevant. The lines referred to by *m* and *n* may also be the same.
Also known as:	Conjunction (CONJ).

Examples.

1	(1)	P	A
2	(2)	Q	A
1,2	(3)	P & Q	1,2 &I
1,2	(4)	Q & P	1,2 &I
1	(5)	P & P	1,1 &I

ampersand-elim   Given a sentence that is a conjunction (at line m), conclude either conjunct.

Annotation: m **&E**
Assumption set: The same as at line m.
Also known as: Simplification (S).

Examples.
(a)

1	(1)	P & Q	A
1	(2)	Q	1 &E
1	(3)	P	1 &E

(b)

1	(1)	P & (Q $\rightarrow$ R)	A
1	(2)	Q $\rightarrow$ R	1 &E

wedge-intro   Given a sentence (at line m), conclude any disjunction having it as a disjunct.

Annotation: m $\vee$**I**
Assumption set: The same as at line m.
Also known as: Addition (ADD).

Examples.

(a)

1	(1)	P	A
1	(2)	P ∨ Q	1 ∨I
1	(3)	(R ↔ ~T) ∨ P	1 ∨I

(b)

| 1 | (1) | Q → R | A |
| 1 | (2) | (Q → R) ∨ (P & ~S) | 1 ∨I |

wedge-elim   Given a sentence (at line m) that is a disjunction and another sentence (at line n) that is a denial of one of its disjuncts conclude the other disjunct.

Annotation:	m, n ∨E
Assumption set:	The union of the assumption sets at lines m and n.
Comment:	The order of m and n in the proof is irrelevant.
Also known as:	Modus Tollendo Ponens (MTP), Disjunctive Syllogism (DS).

Examples.

(a)

1	(1)	P ∨ Q	A
2	(2)	~P	A
1,2	(3)	Q	1,2 ∨E

(b)

1	(1)	P ∨ (Q → R)	A
2	(2)	~(Q → R)	A
1,2	(3)	P	1,2 ∨E

(c)
1	(1)	P ∨ ~R		A
2	(2)	R		A
1,2	(3)	P		1,2 ∨E

arrow-intro   Given a sentence (at line *n*), conclude a conditional having it as the consequent and whose antecedent appears in the proof as an assumption (at line *m*).

Annotation:	**n →I (m)**
Assumption set:	Everything in the assumption set at line *n* excepting *m*, the line number where the antecedent was assumed.
Comment:	The antecedent must be present in the proof as an **assumption**. We speak of **DISCHARGING** this assumption when applying this rule. Placing the number *m* in parentheses indicates it is the discharged assumption. The lines *m* and *n* may be the same.
Also known as:	Conditional Proof (CP).

Examples.
(a)
1	(1)	~P ∨ Q		A
2	(2)	P		A
1,2	(3)	Q		1,2 ∨E
1	(4)	P → Q		3 →I (2)

(b)

1	(1)	R	A
2	(2)	P	A
1	(3)	$P \to R$	$1 \to I$ (2)

(c)

1	(1)	P	A
	(2)	$P \to P$	$1 \to I$ (1)

arrow-elim   Given a conditional sentence (at line m) and another sentence that is its antecedent (at line n), conclude the consequent of the conditional.

Annotation:	$m, n \to E$
Assumption set:	The union of the assumption sets at lines m and n.
Comment:	The order of m and n in the proof is irrelevant.
Also known as:	Modus Ponendo Ponens (MPP), Modus Ponens (MP), Detachment, Affirming the Antecedent.

Example.

1	(1)	$P \to Q$	A
2	(2)	P	A
1,2	(3)	Q	$1,2 \to E$

reductio ad   Given both a sentence and its denial (at lines *m* and *n*),
absurdum   conclude the denial of any assumption appearing in the
                   proof (at line *k*).

    Annotation: ***m, n* RAA (*k*)**

    Assumption set: The union of the assumption sets at
                               m and *n*, excluding *k* (the denied
                               assumption).

    Comment: The sentence at line *k* is the assump-
                               tion discharged (a.k.a. the **REDUC-**
                               TIO ASSUMPTION) and the con-
                               clusion must be a denial of the dis-
                               charged assumption. The sentences
                               at lines *m* and *n* must be denials of
                               each other.

    Also known as: Indirect Proof (IP), ~Intro/ ~Elim.

Examples.

(a)

1	(1)	$P \rightarrow Q$	A
2	(2)	~Q	A
3	(3)	P	A
1,3	(4)	Q	1,3 $\rightarrow$E
1,2	(5)	~P	2,4 RAA (3)

(b)

1	(1)	$P \lor Q$	A
2	(2)	~P	A
3	(3)	~P $\rightarrow$ ~Q	A
2,3	(4)	~Q	2,3 $\rightarrow$E
1,2,3	(5)	P	1,4 $\lor$E
1,3	(6)	P	2,5 RAA (2)

(c)

1	(1)	P	A
2	(2)	Q	A
3	(3)	~Q	A
2,3	(4)	~P	2,3 RAA (1)

double-arrow-intro Given two conditional sentences having the forms $\phi \rightarrow \psi$ and $\psi \rightarrow \phi$ (at lines m and n), conclude a biconditional with ϕ on one side and ψ on the other.

> *Annotation*: $\textbf{\textit{m, n}} \leftrightarrow \textbf{I}$
>
> *Assumption set*: The union of the assumption sets at lines m and n.
>
> *Comment*:   The order of m and n in the proof is irrelevant.

Examples.

1	(1)	$P \rightarrow Q$	A
2	(2)	$Q \rightarrow P$	A
1,2	(3)	$P \leftrightarrow Q$	1,2 $\leftrightarrow$I
1,2	(4)	$Q \leftrightarrow P$	1,2 $\leftrightarrow$I

double-arrow-elim Given a biconditional sentence $\phi \leftrightarrow \psi$ (at line m), conclude either $\phi \rightarrow \psi$ or $\psi \rightarrow \phi$.

> *Annotation*: $\textbf{\textit{m}} \leftrightarrow \textbf{E}$
>
> *Assumption set*: the same as at m.
>
> *Also known as*:   Sometimes the rules $\leftrightarrow$I and $\leftrightarrow$E are subsumed as Definition of Biconditional (df.$\leftrightarrow$).

Examples.

1	(1)	P ↔ Q	A
1	(2)	P → Q	1 ↔E
1	(3)	Q → P	1 ↔E

Comment. These ten rules of proof are truth-preserving. Given true premises, they will always yield true conclusions. This entails that if a proof can be constructed for a given argument, then the argument is valid.

Comment. A number of strategies aid in the discovery of proofs, but there is no substitute for practice. We do not provide any proof-discovery strategies in this book—that is the instructor's job. We do provide plenty of exercises, so there should be no lack of opportunity to practice.

Exercise 1.4.1 Fill in the blanks in the following proofs.

i

P, ~Q ⊢ P & ~Q

1	(1)	P	
	(2)	~Q	A
	(3)	P & ~Q	

ii*

P ∨ Q, ~Q ∨ R,   ⊢

	(1)	P ∨ Q	A
2	(2)	~Q ∨ R	
	(3)		
	(4)	Q	1,3 ∨E
	(5)		2,4

iii* $P \to Q, P \vee Q \vdash Q$

               (1) $P \to Q$ A

               (2) $P \vee Q$ A

3   (3)   ~Q

               (4)   P

               (5)

               (6)   Q   3,5 RAA

iv*   , $\vdash\ \sim P \to R$

               (1) $\sim P \leftrightarrow Q$ A

               (2)   ~P   A

3   (3) $\sim Q \vee R$

               (4) $\sim P \to Q$

               (5)   2,4

               (6)   R

               (7) $\sim P \to R$

v $P \to Q \vdash (R \vee \sim Q) \to (P \to R)$

1   (1) $P \to Q$ A

2   (2)   A

3   (3)   P   A

               (4)   1,3 $\to$E

               (5)   R   2,4 $\vee$E

               (6)   5 $\to$I (3)

1   (7) $(R \vee \sim Q) \to (P \to R)$ 6

Exercise 1.4.2 Give proofs for the following sequents. All of these proofs may be completed without using the rules →I or RAA.

S1*   P ∨ ~R, ~R → S, ~P ⊢ S
S2   P ∨ ~R, ~R → S,~P ⊢ S & ~R
S3*   P → ~Q, ~Q ∨ R → ~S, P & T ⊢ ~S
S4*   P & (Q & R), P & R → ~S, S ∨ T ⊢ T
S5   P → Q, P → R, P ⊢ Q & R
S6   P, Q ∨ R, ~R ∨ S, ~Q ⊢ P & S
S7*   ~P, R ∨ ~P ↔ P ∨ Q ⊢ Q
S8   (P ↔ Q) → R,P → Q,Q → P ⊢ R
S9*   ~P → Q & R, ~P ∨ S → ~T, U & ~P ⊢ (U & R) & ~T
S10   (Q ∨ R) & ~S → T, Q & U, ~S ∨ ~U ⊢ T & U

1.5   **Sequents and Derived Rules**

double   *Comment.* If a sequent has just one sentence on each
turnstile   side of a turnstile, a reversed turnstile may be inserted
                     (⊣) to represent the argument from the sentence on the
                     right to the sentence on the left.

Example. P ⊣⊢ P ∨ P

Comment. This example corresponds to two sequents:
P ⊢ P ∨ P and P ∨ P ⊢ P. You may read the example
as saying 'P therefore P or P, and P or P therefore P'.
When proving ϕ ⊣⊢ ψ, one must give two proofs: one
for ϕ ⊢ ψ and one for ψ ⊢ ϕ.

Example.

Prove P ⊣⊢ P ∨ P.

(a) Prove P ⊢ P ∨ P.

1	(1)	P	A
1	(2)	P ∨ P	1 ∨I

(b) Prove P ∨ P ⊢ P.

1	(1)	P ∨ P	A
2	(2)	~P	A
1,2	(3)	P	1,2 ∨E
1	(4)	P	2,3 RAA (2)

Exercise 1.5.1 Give proofs for the following sequents, using the primitive rules of proof.

S11*	P ⊣⊢ ~~P	**Double Negation**
S12*	P → Q, ~Q ⊢ ~P	**Modus Tollendo Tollens**
S13	P → ~Q, Q ⊢ ~P	**MTT**
S14*	~P → Q, ~Q ⊢ P	**MTT**
S15	~P → ~Q, Q ⊢ P	**MTT**
S16*	P → Q, Q → R ⊢ P → R	**Hypothetical Syllogism**
S17*	P ⊢ Q → P	**True Consequent**
S18*	~P ⊢ P → Q	**False Antecedent**
S19	P ⊢ ~P → Q	**FA**
S20	P → Q, P → ~ Q ⊢ ~P	**Impossible Antecedent**
S21*	~P ∨ Q ⊣⊢ P → Q	**Wedge-Arrow (∨→)**
S22	P ∨ Q ⊣⊢ ~P → Q	∨→
S23	P ∨ Q ⊣⊢ ~Q → P	∨→
S24	P ∨ ~Q ⊣⊢ Q → P	∨→
S25	P ∨ Q, P → R, Q → R ⊢ R	**Simple Dilemma**

S26*	$P \vee Q, P \rightarrow R, Q \rightarrow S \vdash R \vee S$	**Complex Di**lemma
S27	$P \rightarrow Q, {\sim}P \rightarrow Q \vdash Q$	**Spec**ial **Di**lemma
S28*	${\sim}(P \vee Q) \dashv\vdash {\sim}P \,\&\, {\sim}Q$	**De**Morgan's Law
S29	${\sim}(P \,\&\, Q) \dashv\vdash {\sim}P \vee {\sim}Q$	DM
S30	$P \,\&\, Q \dashv\vdash {\sim}({\sim}P \vee {\sim}Q)$	DM
S31	$P \vee Q \dashv\vdash {\sim}({\sim}P \,\&\, {\sim}Q)$	DM
S32*	${\sim}(P \rightarrow Q) \dashv\vdash P \,\&\, {\sim}Q$	Negated Arrow (Neg$\rightarrow$)
S33	${\sim}(P \rightarrow {\sim}Q) \dashv\vdash P \,\&\, Q$	Neg$\rightarrow$
S34	$P \rightarrow Q \dashv\vdash {\sim}(P \,\&\, {\sim}Q)$	Neg$\rightarrow$
S35	$P \rightarrow {\sim}Q \dashv\vdash {\sim}(P \,\&\, Q)$	Neg$\rightarrow$
S36	$P \,\&\, Q \dashv\vdash Q \,\&\, P$	**& Commu**tativity
S37*	$P \vee Q \dashv\vdash Q \vee P$	$\vee$ **Commu**tativity
S38*	$P \leftrightarrow Q \dashv\vdash Q \leftrightarrow P$	$\leftrightarrow$ **Commu**tativity
S39	$P \rightarrow Q \dashv\vdash {\sim}Q \rightarrow {\sim}P$	**Trans**position
S40	$P \,\&\, (Q \,\&\, R) \dashv\vdash (P \,\&\, Q) \,\&\, R$	**& Associ**ativity
S41*	$P \vee (Q \vee R) \dashv\vdash (P \vee Q) \vee R$	$\vee$ **Associ**ativity
S42*	$P \,\&\, (Q \vee R) \dashv\vdash (P \,\&\, Q) \vee (P \,\&\, R)$	**&/$\vee$ Distr**ibution
S43	$P \vee (Q \,\&\, R) \dashv\vdash (P \vee Q) \,\&\, (P \vee R)$	$\vee$**/& Distr**ibution
S44	$P \rightarrow (Q \rightarrow R) \dashv\vdash P \,\&\, Q \rightarrow R$	**Imp/Exp**ortation
S45	$P \leftrightarrow Q, P \vdash Q$	**Biconditional Ponens**
S46	$P \leftrightarrow Q, Q \vdash P$	BP
S47	$P \leftrightarrow Q, {\sim}P \vdash {\sim}Q$	**Biconditional Tollens**
S48	$P \leftrightarrow Q, {\sim}Q \vdash {\sim}P$	BT
S49	$P \leftrightarrow Q \dashv\vdash {\sim}Q \leftrightarrow {\sim}P$	**BiTrans**position
S50	$P \leftrightarrow {\sim}Q \dashv\vdash {\sim}P \leftrightarrow Q$	BiTrans
S51	${\sim}(P \leftrightarrow Q) \dashv\vdash P \leftrightarrow {\sim}Q$	**Neg**ated $\leftrightarrow$
S52	${\sim}(P \leftrightarrow Q) \dashv\vdash {\sim}P \leftrightarrow Q$	**Neg**$\leftrightarrow$

Exercise 1.5.2 Give proofs for the following sequents using the primitive rules of proof.

S53*   P ↔ Q ⊣⊢ (P & Q) ∨ (~P & ~Q)

S54   P → Q & R, R ∨ ~Q → S & T, T ↔ U ⊢ P → U

S55*   (~P ∨ Q) & R, Q → S ⊢ P → (R → S)

S56*   Q & R, Q → P ∨ S, ~(S & R) ⊢ P

S57   P → R & Q, S → ~R ∨ ~Q ⊢ S & P → T

S58   R & P, R → (S ∨ Q), ~(Q & P) ⊢ S

S59   P & Q, R & ~S, Q → (P → T), T→(R→S∨W) ⊢ W

S60   R → ~P, Q, Q → (P ∨ ~S) ⊢ S → ~R

S61   P → Q, P → R, P → S, T → (U → (~V → ~S)),
                 Q → T, R → (W → U), V → ~W, W ⊢ ~P

S62   P ↔ ~Q & S, P & (~T → ~S) ⊢ ~Q & T

S63   P ∨ Q ↔ P & Q ⊢ P ↔ Q

substitution   *Definition.* A **SUBSTITUTION INSTANCE** of a
instance   sequent is the result of uniformly replacing its
                    sentence letters with wffs.

Comment. This definition states that each occurrence of a given sentence letter must be replaced with the same wff throughout the sequent.

Example.
The sequent
        P ∨ Q ⊢ ~P → Q
has as a substitution instance the sequent
        (R & S) ∨ Q ⊢ ~(R & S) → Q
according to the substitution pattern
        P/(R & S); Q/Q.

Comment. The given substitution pattern shows that the sentence letter P was replaced throughout the original sequent by the wff (R & S), and the sentence letter Q was replaced throughout by itself.

Exercise 1.5.3 Identify each of the following with a sequent in exercise 1.5.1 and identify the substitution pattern.

i*   R → S ⊣⊢ ~S → ~R

ii*   ~P → Q ∨ R, Q ∨ R → S ⊢ ~P → S

iii*   (P & Q) ∨ R ⊣⊢ R ∨ (P & Q)

iv*   (P ∨ Q) & (~R ∨ ~S) ⊣⊢ ((P ∨ Q) & ~R) ∨ ((P ∨ Q) & ~S)

v*   R ∨ S ⊣⊢ ~~(R ∨ S)

vi*   (P ∨ R) & S ⊣⊢ ~(P ∨ R → ~S)

vii*   P ∨ (Q ∨ R) ⊣⊢ ~P → Q ∨ R

viii*   ~(P & Q) ⊢ R → ~(P & Q)

ix*   ~((P & Q) ∨ (R & S)) ⊣⊢ ~(P & Q) & ~(R & S)

x*   P ∨ (R ∨ S), P → Q & R, R ∨ S → Q & R ⊢ Q & R

derived rule *Comment.* Any sequent that one has proved using only the primitive rules may subsequently be used as a **DERIVED RULE** of proof if

(i) some sentences appearing in the proof are the premises of the sequent, or

(ii) some sentences appearing in the proof are the premises of a substitution instance of the sequent.

In case (i) the conclusion of the sequent may be asserted on the current line; in case (ii) the conclusion *of the substitution instance* may be asserted.

Annotation: The line numbers of the premises fol-
                        lowed by S#, where S# is the num-
                        ber from the book, or the name of
                        the sequent (see comment below).

Assumption set: The union of the assumption sets of
                        the premises.

Comment. All of the sequents in exercise 1.5.1 (S11–
S52) are used so frequently as rules of proof that they
have the names we have indicated. (Indeed, in some
systems of logic some of our derived rules are given as
primitive rules.)

Examples.

(a) Prove R ∨ S → T, ~T ⊢ ~R.

1	(1)	R ∨ S → T	A
2	(2)	~T	A
1,2	(3)	~(R ∨ S)	1,2 MTT
1,2	(4)	~R & ~S	3 DM
1,2	(5)	~R	4 &E

(b) Prove P ∨ R → S, T → ~S ⊢ T → ~(P ∨ R).

1	(1)	P ∨ R → S	A
2	(2)	T → ~S	A
1	(3)	~S → ~(P ∨ R)	1 Trans
1,2	(4)	T → ~(P ∨ R)	2,3 HS

Comment. Requiring that the sequent to be used as a derived rule has been proved using only primitive rules is unnecessarily restrictive. If the sequents are proved in a strict order and no later sequent in the series is used in the proof of an earlier sequent, then no logical errors can result. We suggest the stronger restriction only because it is good practice to construct proofs using only the primitive rules.

Exercise 1.5.4 Prove the following using either primitive or derived rules from the previous exercises. If you like a challenge, prove them again using primitive rules only.

S64	$\sim P \to P \dashv\vdash P$
S65	$P \leftrightarrow Q \dashv\vdash \sim((P \to Q) \to \sim(Q \to P))$
S66*	$P \leftrightarrow Q \dashv\vdash P \lor Q \to P \& Q$
S67*	$P \leftrightarrow Q \dashv\vdash \sim(P \lor Q) \lor \sim(\sim P \lor \sim Q)$
S68	$P \leftrightarrow Q \dashv\vdash \sim(P \& Q) \to \sim(P \lor Q)$
S69	$P \leftrightarrow Q \dashv\vdash \sim(\sim(P \& Q) \& \sim(\sim P \& \sim Q))$
S70	$P \lor Q \to R \& \sim P, Q \lor R, \sim R \vdash C$
S71	$\sim P \leftrightarrow Q, P \to R, \sim R \vdash \sim Q \leftrightarrow R$
S72	$\sim((P \leftrightarrow \sim Q) \leftrightarrow R), S \to P \& (Q \& T),$
	$\qquad\qquad\qquad R \lor (P \& S) \vdash S \& K \to R \& Q$
S73*	$(P \& Q) \lor (R \lor S) \vdash ((P \& Q) \lor R) \lor S$
S74	$P \& (\sim Q \& \sim R), P \to (\sim S \to T), \sim S \to (T \leftrightarrow R \lor Q) \vdash S$
S75	$P \& \sim Q \to \sim R, (\sim S \to \sim P) \leftrightarrow \sim R \vdash R \leftrightarrow Q \& (P \& \sim S)$
S76*	$P \lor Q, (Q \to R) \& (\sim P \lor S), Q \& R \to T \vdash T \lor S$
S77	$P \to Q \lor R, (\sim Q \& S) \lor (T \to \sim P), \sim(\sim R \to \sim P) \vdash \sim T \& Q$
S78*	$P \lor Q, P \to (R \to \sim S), (\sim R \leftrightarrow T) \to \sim P \vdash S \& T \to Q$
S79*	$(P \leftrightarrow \sim Q) \to \sim R, (\sim P \& S) \lor (Q \& T), S \lor T \to R \vdash Q \to P$
S80*	$\sim S \lor (S \& R), (S \to R) \to P \vdash P$
S81*	$P \lor (R \lor Q), (R \to S) \& (Q \to T), S \lor T \to P \lor Q, \sim P \vdash Q$

S82* $(P \rightarrow Q) \rightarrow R, S \rightarrow (\sim Q \rightarrow T) \vdash R \vee \sim T \rightarrow (S \rightarrow R)$

S83* $P \& Q \rightarrow R \vee S \vdash (P \rightarrow R) \vee (Q \rightarrow S)$

S84* $(P \rightarrow Q) \& (R \rightarrow P), (P \vee R) \& \sim(Q\&R) \vdash (P\&Q) \& \sim R$

S85* $P \& Q \rightarrow (R \vee S) \& \sim(R \& S), R \& Q \rightarrow S,$

                     $S \rightarrow ((R \& Q) \vee (\sim R \& \sim Q)) \vee \sim P \vdash P \rightarrow \sim Q$

S86 $\sim(P \& \sim Q) \vee \sim(\sim R \& \sim S), \sim S \& \sim Q, T \rightarrow (\sim S \rightarrow \sim R \& P) \vdash \sim T$

1.6   Theorems

theorem   *Definition.* A **THEOREM** is a sentence that can be proved from the empty set of premises.

Comment. We can assert that a given sentence is a theorem by presenting it as the conclusion of a sequent with nothing to the left of the turnstile.

Example.
Prove $\vdash P \& Q \rightarrow Q \& P$.

1	(1)	P & Q	A
1	(2)	Q	1 &E
1	(3)	P	1 &E
1	(4)	Q & P	2,3 &I
	(5)	P & Q → Q & P	4 →I (1)

Comment. Note that in step 5 we discharge assumption 1. Hence, the final conclusion rests on no assumptions.

Exercise 1.6.1 Prove the following theorems, (i) using primitive rules only and (ii) using primitive rules together with derived rules established in a previous exercise.

T1*	⊢ P → P	**Id**entity
T2*	⊢ P ∨ ~P	**Excluded Middle**
T3	⊢ ~(P & ~P)	Non-Contradiction
T4*	⊢ P → (Q → P)	**Weak**ening
T5*	⊢ (P → Q) ∨ (Q → P)	**Paradox of Material Implication**
T6	⊢ P ↔ ~~P	**Double Negation**
T7	⊢ (P ↔ Q) ↔ (Q ↔ P)	
T8*	⊢ ~(P ↔ Q) ↔ (~P ↔ Q)	
T9*	⊢ ((P → Q) → P) → P	**Peirce's Law**
T10*	⊢ (P → Q) ∨ (Q → R)	
T11*	⊢ (P ↔ Q) ↔ (~ P ↔ ~Q)	
T12*	⊢ (~P → Q) & (R → Q) ↔ (P → R) → Q	
T13*	⊢ P ↔ P & P	**& Idem**potence
T14*	⊢ P ↔ P ∨ P	**∨ Idem**potence
T15	⊢ (P ↔ Q) & (R ↔ S) → ((P → R) ↔ (Q → S))	
T16	⊢ (P ↔ Q) & (R ↔ S) → (P & R ↔ Q & S)	
T17*	⊢ (P ↔ Q) & (R ↔ S) → (P ∨ R ↔ Q ∨ S)	
T18	⊢ (P ↔ Q) & (R ↔ S) → ((P ↔ R) ↔ (Q ↔ S))	
T19*	⊢ (P↔Q) →((R→P)↔(R→Q)) & ((P→R)↔(Q→R))	
T20	⊢ (P ↔ Q) → (R & P ↔ R & Q)	
T21*	⊢ (P ↔ Q) → (R ∨ P ↔ R ∨ Q)	
T22	⊢ (P ↔ Q) → ((R ↔ P) ↔ (R ↔ Q))	
T23	⊢ P & (Q ↔ R) → (P & Q ↔ R)	
T24	⊢ P → (Q → R) ↔ ((P → Q) → (P → R))	
T25	⊢ P → (Q → R) ↔ Q → (P → R)	
T26	⊢ P → (P → Q) ↔ P → Q	
T27*	⊢ (P → Q) → Q ↔ (Q → P) → P	

T28 $\vdash P \rightarrow {\sim}Q \leftrightarrow Q \rightarrow {\sim}P$

T29 $\vdash {\sim}P \rightarrow P \leftrightarrow P$

T30* $\vdash (P \mathbin{\&} Q) \vee (R \mathbin{\&} S) \leftrightarrow$
$$((P \vee R) \mathbin{\&} (P \vee S)) \mathbin{\&} ((Q \vee R) \mathbin{\&} (Q \vee S))$$

T31* $\vdash (P \vee Q) \mathbin{\&} (R \vee S) \leftrightarrow$
$$((P \mathbin{\&} R) \vee (P \mathbin{\&} S)) \vee ((Q \mathbin{\&} R) \vee (Q \mathbin{\&} S))$$

T32* $\vdash (P \rightarrow Q) \mathbin{\&} (R \rightarrow S) \leftrightarrow$
$$(({\sim}P \mathbin{\&} {\sim}R) \vee ({\sim}P \mathbin{\&} S)) \vee ((Q \mathbin{\&} {\sim}R) \vee (Q \mathbin{\&} S))$$

T33 $\vdash (P \vee {\sim}P) \mathbin{\&} Q \leftrightarrow Q$

T34 $\vdash (P \mathbin{\&} {\sim}P) \vee Q \leftrightarrow Q$

T35 $\vdash P \vee ({\sim}P \mathbin{\&} Q) \leftrightarrow P \vee Q$

T36 $\vdash P \mathbin{\&} ({\sim}P \vee Q) \leftrightarrow P \mathbin{\&} Q$

T37 $\vdash P \leftrightarrow P \vee (P \mathbin{\&} Q)$

T38 $\vdash P \leftrightarrow P \mathbin{\&} (P \vee Q)$

T39 $\vdash (P \rightarrow Q \mathbin{\&} R) \rightarrow (P \mathbin{\&} Q \leftrightarrow P \mathbin{\&} R)$

theorems as derived rules

Comment. We now consider a special case of the use of sequents as derived rules. Since it is the conclusion of a sequent without premises, a theorem or a substitution instance of a theorem can be written as a line of a proof with an empty assumption set. For a theorem to be used this way, it must have been proved already by means of primitive rules alone. The annotation should be the name of the theorem or T# (the theorem's number).

Example.

Prove P → Q, ~P → Q ⊢ Q.

1	(1)	P → Q	A
2	(2)	~P → Q	A
	(3)	P ∨ ~P	T2
1,2	(4)	Q	1,2,3 SimDil

Comment. In the preceding example, the annotation for line 3 gives the number of the theorem introduced. Since this theorem has a name, the annotation 'Excluded Middle' would also have been acceptable.

Comment. As with sequent introductions, requiring that theorems first be proved using only primitive rules is unnecessarily restrictive.

Exercise 1.6.2 Using theorems as derived rules, attempt to construct alternative proofs of sequents appearing in exercise 1.5.4.

Chapter 2
Truth Tables

2.1 **Truth Tables for Sentences**

truth value *Definition.* Truth and Falsity (abbreviated **T** and **F**) are **TRUTH VALUES.**

truth table *Comment.* When an argument is valid, its conclusion cannot be false when its premises are all true. One way to discover whether an argument is valid is to consider explicitly *all the possible combinations* of truth values among the premises and the conclusion. In this chapter we show how to do this. The idea is to assign truth values variously to the sentence letters of the argument and see how the premises and the conclusion turn out. The following rules, codified in **TRUTH TABLES** (TTs), enable us to do this.

Comment. For this method to work, it has to be the case that the truth values of compound sentences are determined by the truth values of the sentence letters that appear in them.

truth-functional connectives *Comment.* All the sentential connectives introduced in chapter 1 have the property described in the previous comment. Since the truth values of compound sentences containing these connectives are *functions* of the truth values of the component wffs, they are known as **TRUTH-FUNCTIONAL CONNECTIVES.** (Not all English connectives are truth-functional.)

TT for negation In order for a negation ~ϕ to be true, ϕ must be false.

ϕ	~ϕ
T	F
F	T

Table 2.1 Truth function for negation.

TT for conjunction   In order for a conjunction (ϕ & ψ) to be true, both conjuncts ϕ and ψ must be true.

TT for disjunction   In order for a disjunction (ϕ ∨ ψ) to be false, both disjuncts ϕ and ψ must be false.

TT for conditional   In order for a conditional (ϕ → ψ) to be false, the antecedent ϕ must be true while the consequent ψ is false.

TT for biconditional   In order for a biconditional (ϕ ↔ ψ) to be true, ϕ and ψ must have the same truth value.

ϕ	ψ	ϕ & ψ	ϕ ∨ ψ	ϕ → ψ	ϕ ↔ ψ
T	T	T	T	T	T
T	F	F	T	F	F
F	T	F	T	T	F
F	F	F	F	T	T

Table 2.2 Truth functions for the binary connectives.

Comment. Observe that if a conditional's antecedent is false, then the conditional is true no matter what the truth value of its consequent. Also, if its consequent is true, then it is true, regardless of the truth value of its antecedent. These are the truth table analogues of the derived rules False Antecedent and True Consequent.

TTs for sentences

By means of these rules we can construct TTs for compound wffs, exhibiting how their truth values are determined by the truth values of their sentence letters.

Example.

P Q R	(P $\rightarrow$ Q) v (~Q & R)			
T T T	T	T	F	F
T T F	T	T	F	F
T F T	F	T	T	T
T F F	F	F	T	F
F T T	T	T	F	F
F T F	T	T	F	F
F F T	T	T	T	T
F F F	T	T	T	F
	(a)	*(d)*	*(b)*	*(c)*

Table 2.3 *TT for the sentence (P $\rightarrow$ Q) v (~Q & R).*

Comment. By referring to the columns for P and Q, we construct column (a), for (P → Q), using the TT for conditionals (see table 2.2). Next, we construct column (b), for ~Q, (see table 2.1). Column (c), for (~Q & R) is constructed by referring to the columns for its conjuncts, ~Q and R and using the TT for conjunction (see table 2.2). Finally, we construct column (d), for (P → Q) ∨ (~Q & R), by referring to those for its disjuncts, (P → Q) and (~Q & R) (see table 2.2).

Comment. The column for a given component of a sentence (other than the sentence letters) is placed under that component's connective. For example, the column for (P → Q) in table 2.3 falls under its arrow.

Exercise 2.1   Construct TTs for the following sentences.

i*	P ∨ (~P ∨ Q)
ii*	~(P & Q) ∨ P
iii*	~(P → Q) → P
iv*	(P ∨ Q) ∨ (~P & Q)
v*	P ∨ Q → R ∨ ~P
vi*	R ↔ ~P ∨ (R & Q)
vii*	(P & Q ↔ Q) → (Q → P)
viii*	(P ↔ ~Q) ↔ (~P ↔ ~Q)
ix*	(P ↔ Q) ↔ (P ∨ R → (~Q → R))
x*	(P & Q) ∨ (R & S) → (P & R) ∨ (Q & S)

For additional practice, construct TTs for wffs in chapter 1.

| 2.2 | **Truth Tables for Sequents** |

**validity
with TTs**

To determine a sequent's validity or invalidity, we construct a single TT for the whole sequent. If there is a line in the TT where all the premises are true and the conclusion is false, then the sequent is invalid. If there is no such line, it is valid.

P Q	~P, Q → (P & Q) ⊢ ~Q
T T	F T T F
T F	F T F T
F T	T F F F
F F	T T F T

valid example

Table 2.4 *This sequent is valid since there is no line on which ~P and Q → (P & Q) are both true but ~Q is false.*

P Q R	~P → Q,	(R & P) → Q	⊢ Q
T T T	F T	T T	
T T F	F T	F T	
T F T	F T	T F	
T F F	F T	F T	
F T T	T T	F T	
F T F	T T	F T	
F F T	T F	F T	
F F F	T F	F T	

invalid example

Table 2.5 *This sequent is invalid since there is at least one line where ~P → Q and (R & P) → Q are both true but the conclusion is false—the fourth line.*

invalidating assignment

Definition. An **INVALIDATING ASSIGNMENT** for a sequent is an assignment of truth and falsity to its sentence letters that makes the premises true and the conclusion false.

Comment. From the TT for an invalid sequent, you can read off an invalidating assignment. Find a row of the TT where the premises are all true and the conclusion is false. The invalidating assignment is given at the left side of that row.

Example.
An invalidating assignment for the sequent in Table 2.5 assigns truth to P and falsity to Q and R.

number
of lines

Comment. When the sequent in question involves only two sentence letters, the TT has exactly four lines; three sentence letters requires eight lines. In general, when *n* sentence letters are present, the number of lines in the TT is 2^n.

incompatible
premises

Comment. Consider this special case:If you construct a TT for the sequent $P \rightarrow Q$, $Q \rightarrow R$, $P \& \sim R \vdash S$ you find that there is no line on which all the premises are true. Consequently, there is no line on which the conclusion is false while all the premises are true. Thus the sequent is valid.

Exercise 2.2

Use TTs to determine whether each of the following sequents is valid. For each invalid one, find an invalidating assignment. For each valid one, give a proof.

i*	$P \& \sim Q \vdash \sim (P \leftrightarrow Q)$
ii*	$P \& (Q \vee R) \vdash Q \& (P \vee R)$
iii*	$P \& Q \rightarrow R \vdash P \rightarrow R$
iv*	$P \vee Q \rightarrow R \vdash P \rightarrow R$
v*	$P \rightarrow Q \vee R \vdash P \rightarrow R$
vi*	$(P \rightarrow \sim P) \rightarrow (\sim P \rightarrow P) \vdash P$
vii*	$Q \rightarrow R \vdash (P \rightarrow Q) \& (Q \rightarrow R)$
viii*	$P \vee Q, P \rightarrow R, \sim S \rightarrow \sim Q \vdash \sim P$
ix*	$P \rightarrow Q, P \rightarrow R, \sim (\sim R \rightarrow Q) \vdash P$
x*	$P \leftrightarrow \sim Q, Q \leftrightarrow \sim R, R \leftrightarrow \sim S \vdash P \leftrightarrow S$
xi*	$P \vee Q \vdash (\sim P \rightarrow R) \vee (\sim Q \rightarrow R)$
xii*	$P \leftrightarrow (R \rightarrow P \vee \sim Q), \sim (R \rightarrow P \vee Q) \vdash \sim Q$
xiii*	$\sim (R \& \sim P \rightarrow Q \vee R) \vdash \sim (Q \leftrightarrow R)$
xiv*	$P \rightarrow (Q \& R \rightarrow S), P, \sim S \vdash \sim (Q \& R)$

xv*   ~R → ~Q, (~P & R) → ~Q ⊢ ~(P ↔ ~R & Q)

xvi*   S→(T↔P), Q→(~S↔~T), ~(P&R↔T→S)⊢ R & ~Q

xvii*   Q → (P → R & ~Q), ~Q → ~(T ∨ V), U & S ↔ P
                                                              ⊢ (S → ~U) ∨ ~T

xviii*   Q ∨ R → U & T, ~(P ↔ Q), ~(S ∨ W) → P
                                            ⊢ Q ∨ V → (S & U) ∨ (T & W)

2.3   Tautologies

no premises   *Comment.* Another special case is a valid sequent
                without premises. In this case, validity requires that
                there be no lines of the TT on which the conclusion is
                false, since no premises are present to be considered.

P Q	⊢ P → (~P → Q)
T T	T F T
T F	T F T
F T	T T T
F F	T T F

Table 2.6 A valid sequent without premises.

P Q R	⊢ (P ↔ Q) → (P ∨ ~R)
T T T	T T T F
T T F	T T T T
T F T	F T T F
T F F	F T T T
F T T	F T F F
F T F	F T T T
F F T	T F F F
F F F	T T T T

Table 2.7 *An invalid sequent without premises.*

tautology

Definition. A sentence φ is a **TAUTOLOGY** (or, is **TAUTOLOGOUS**) when the sequent that has no premises and has φ as its conclusion is valid.

Comment. When a sentence is a tautology, it cannot be false: its TT has only Ts in the column for the sentence. Some sentences have only Fs appearing in their column of a TT; others have both Ts and Fs. The sentence appearing in table 2.6 is a tautology.

inconsistent and contingent

Definition. A sentence that has only Fs in its column of a TT is **INCONSISTENT.** A sentence that is neither tautologous nor inconsistent is **CONTINGENT.**

Comment. The sentence appearing in table 2.7 is contingent.

P	P & ~P	P v ~P
T F	F F F T	T F T T

Table 2.8 *P is contingent, P & ~P is inconsistent,
and P ∨ ~P is tautologous.*

P Q	((P → Q) → P) → P
T T T F F T F F	T T T F T T T F T T F T

Table 2.9 *((P → Q) → P) → P is tautologous.*

P Q	(P & Q) ↔ (~P ∨ ~Q)
T T	T F F F F
T F	F F F T T
F T	F F T T F
F F	F F T T T

Table 2.10 *(P & Q) ↔ (~P ∨ ~Q) is inconsistent.*

Exercise 2.3   Use TTs to establish that all the theorems considered in chapter 1 are tautologies.

2.4   Indirect TTs

indirect TT   *Comment.* TTs provide a way to search systematically for invalidating assignments. A shorter way of doing this is the indirect truth table (ITT).

In an ITT, one attempts to build invalidating assignments. When the sequent is valid, it is impossible to build an invalidating assignment (as in the first example below).

In cases of invalid arguments, an invalidating assignment can be discovered (as in the second example below). Sometimes one must examine more than one assignment (as in the third example below).

easy valid case Example.

Consider the sequent

P → Q, ~R → ~Q ⊢ ~R → ~P

There is only way for the conclusion (~R → ~P) to be false: ~R must be true and ~P false. That is, R must be false and P must be true, as shown below.

P → Q, ~R → ~Q ⊢ ~R → ~P
T   TF   TF *F* FT

Having established these truth assignments, we now see if there is any way of making the premises all true that is compatible with this assignment. In other words, we need a value of Q to complete the following:

P → Q, ~R → ~Q ⊢ ~R → ~P
T *T*   TF *T*   TF *F* FT

The assignment indicated requires Q to be true, in order for the first premise to be true, but also requires ~Q to be true (hence Q to be false), in order for the second premise to be true. This is the only way to make both premises true and the conclusion false, and it is impossible to achieve. Thus, there are no invalidating assignments, and the argument is valid.

easy
invalid case

Example.

The sequent below has a conditional conclusion. Thus, if the conclusion is to be false, its antecedent must be true and its consequent false.

P & ~Q,   Q → R ⊢ P → R
T *T* TF   F *T* F   T *F* F

The invalidating assignment assigns T to P and F to Q and R.

harder case

Example.

In the sequent below there are three ways to make the conclusion false. Here is one of them:

~P → Q, ~P → ~Q   ⊢   P & Q
                                      F *F* T

On this assignment, the second premise is false. Thus, we have failed to find an invalidating assignment. So we try a different way of making P & Q false:

~P → Q,   ~P → ~Q   ⊢   P & Q
FT   FT   T *F* F

Here, both premises are true, since they both have false antecedents. Thus, an invalidating assignment assigns T to P and F to Q.

Exercise 2.4.1 Use ITTs to determine whether the sequents given in exercise 2.2 are valid or invalid.

Exercise 2.4.2 Use ITTs to determine whether the following sequents are valid. For each invalid one, give an invalidating assignment. For each valid one, construct a proof.

i*	$P \rightarrow Q, Q \vdash P$
ii*	$P \vee Q, P \vdash Q$
iii*	$P \rightarrow Q, {\sim}Q \rightarrow R \vdash P \rightarrow R$
iv*	$P \vee {\sim}Q, {\sim}Q \& R \vdash P \& R$
v*	$P \leftrightarrow Q \vee R, {\sim}Q \vdash {\sim}P$
vi*	$P \rightarrow Q, (R \rightarrow S) \rightarrow {\sim}P \vdash Q \vee R$
vii*	$P \rightarrow Q \vee R, Q \rightarrow S \& T, {\sim}S \vdash {\sim}P$
viii*	$P \& {\sim}Q \rightarrow R, P \leftrightarrow {\sim}R \vdash (Q \& R) \vee P$
ix*	$P \rightarrow Q \& {\sim}R, {\sim}P \vee Q \leftrightarrow S \vdash S \rightarrow {\sim}P \vee T$
x*	${\sim}(P \leftrightarrow Q), P \rightarrow R, Q \rightarrow S \vdash {\sim}R \vee S$
xi*	$S \rightarrow Q, {\sim}S \rightarrow Q \vee T, T \rightarrow P \vdash P \rightarrow Q \vee R$
xii*	${\sim}Q \rightarrow S, S \rightarrow Q \vee {\sim}T, {\sim}T \rightarrow P \vdash Q \rightarrow P \vee R$
xiii*	$P \rightarrow ({\sim}Q \rightarrow {\sim}R \& {\sim}S), {\sim}(R \leftrightarrow S), {\sim}Q \vdash {\sim}P$
xiv*	$P \vee Q, {\sim}(R \rightarrow P) \vdash Q \leftrightarrow ({\sim}T \rightarrow {\sim}R \vee S)$
xv*	$P \& S \rightarrow R, R \vee T, T \rightarrow Q \& P, {\sim}Q \vee U \vdash P \rightarrow S \vee U$
xvi*	${\sim}(P \leftrightarrow Q), P \rightarrow R, Q \rightarrow S \vdash {\sim}R \vee S$
xvii*	${\sim}(P \rightarrow {\sim}Q \& R), {\sim}R \leftrightarrow {\sim}P \vdash P \& Q$
xviii*	$(P \rightarrow Q) \& ({\sim}Q \rightarrow P \& R) \rightarrow (S \vee T \rightarrow {\sim}Q)$
	$\vdash Q \rightarrow {\sim}({\sim}S \rightarrow T)$
xix*	$\vdash (P \vee {\sim}Q \rightarrow {\sim}P \& {\sim}Q) \leftrightarrow {\sim}P$
xx*	$Q \leftrightarrow {\sim}Q \vdash P \leftrightarrow {\sim}P$

2.5   English Counterexamples

counter-
example

Definition. An English **COUNTEREXAMPLE** for an invalid argument or sequent is an argument that has the same logical form as the original, but whose premises are all *obviously* true and whose conclusion is *obviously* false.

Example.
A counterexample for $P \rightarrow Q, Q \vdash P$ is

If Los Angeles is in Canada, then Los Angeles is in North America.
Los Angeles is in North America.
Therefore, Los Angeles is in Canada.

Comment. The relationships of Los Angeles, Canada, and North America to one another are public knowledge. The premises are both obviously true, and the conclusion is obviously false.

Comment. In constructing a counterexample, it is not generally useful to construct the premises and the conclusion using either unspecific pronouns or personal information. For example, given the invalid sequent above, one might present

If it is raining then there are clouds in the sky.
There are clouds in the sky.
Therefore, it is raining.

Although one can see in a hypothetical situation that the premises might be true at the same time as the conclusion is false, the trouble with this argument as a counterexample is that the second premise is not *obviously* true (you may not be in a position to determine whether there are clouds in the sky) and likewise the conclusion is not *obviously* false.

Similarly, the following is not useful:

If my cousin is intelligent, she will pass logic.
My cousin will pass logic.
Therefore, my cousin is intelligent.

Since it is not general knowledge who your cousin is and whether or not she is intelligent or will pass logic, this does not provide a clear counterexample to the given sequent.

Exercise 2.5.1 Construct counterexamples for the invalid sequents in chapter 2.

Exercise 2.5.2 Give proofs, invalidating assignments, or counterexamples to establish the validity or the invalidity of the following sequents:

i $P \rightarrow Q, \sim Q \vee R, R \vdash P$
ii $\sim P \vee Q, \sim Q \vee R, \sim R \vdash \sim P$
iii $P \leftrightarrow Q, Q \leftrightarrow \sim R \vdash \sim P \leftrightarrow \sim R$

iv $(Q \rightarrow P) \rightarrow R, \sim Q \vee S, \sim S \vdash \sim R \rightarrow T$

v $P \& (Q \rightarrow R), Q \vee \sim P, R \vee S \rightarrow T \vdash T \vee U$

vi $P \leftrightarrow \sim Q, R \vee \sim Q, R \leftrightarrow S \vdash S \vee P$

vii $P \leftrightarrow Q, Q \leftrightarrow \sim R, R \rightarrow P \vdash \sim P \leftrightarrow \sim R$

viii $P \leftrightarrow Q \vdash (R \leftrightarrow P) \leftrightarrow (P \leftrightarrow Q)$

ix $\sim R \leftrightarrow \sim Q, P \vee \sim Q, P \leftrightarrow S \vdash S \vee \sim R$

x $R \leftrightarrow \sim Q, P \vee \sim Q, P \leftrightarrow S \vdash S \& R$

xi $(P \rightarrow Q) \vee (R \rightarrow S) \vdash (P \rightarrow S) \vee (R \rightarrow Q)$

xii $(P \rightarrow Q) \& (R \rightarrow S) \vdash (P \rightarrow S) \& (R \rightarrow Q)$

xiii $P \& Q, Q \rightarrow (R \rightarrow P), R \rightarrow (\sim S \rightarrow \sim T \vee \sim W), \sim S \& T \vdash W$

xiv $P \& Q, Q \rightarrow (P \rightarrow R), R \rightarrow (\sim S \rightarrow \sim T \vee \sim W), \sim S \& T \vdash \sim W$

xv $P \vee Q \rightarrow R \vee S, \sim (T \vee R) \rightarrow S, (T \rightarrow P) \& (R \rightarrow Q), \sim S \vdash R$

xvi $\sim (P \vee \sim Q), \sim P \rightarrow R \vee S, \sim S \vee \sim Q,$

                       $R \vee \sim T \rightarrow W \& (Y \rightarrow \sim Q) \vdash \sim (W \rightarrow Y)$

xvii $P \vee (Q \vee R), S \& \sim T, \sim (\sim S \vee T) \rightarrow \sim P, (R \rightarrow W) \& \sim W \vdash Q$

xviii $P \vee (Q \vee R), S \& \sim T, (R \rightarrow W) \& \sim W \vdash Q$

xix $(P \leftrightarrow Q) \leftrightarrow (\sim P \leftrightarrow \sim R) \vdash P \rightarrow (Q \leftrightarrow R)$

xx $P \leftrightarrow Q, \sim (\sim R \& P), R \vee S \rightarrow \sim (T \& Q) \vdash T \rightarrow \sim (P \vee Q)$

xxi $P \leftrightarrow Q, R \vee \sim P, T \& Q \rightarrow \sim R \vdash \sim S \& T \rightarrow \sim (P \vee Q)$

xxii $P \& Q \rightarrow (R \leftrightarrow S), \sim P \rightarrow \sim T, \sim (\sim R \vee S) \vdash Q \rightarrow \sim T$

xxiii $P \& Q \rightarrow R, P \& \sim R \leftrightarrow Q \vee \sim S,$

          $T \& (\sim Q \& \sim R \rightarrow P), (T \rightarrow S) \vee (T \rightarrow R) \vdash S \& R$

xxiv $R \vee (P \rightarrow S), T \& \sim W, (\sim T \vee W) \rightarrow \sim R, (S \rightarrow Q) \& \sim Q \vdash \sim P$

xxv $R \vee (P \vee S), T \& \sim W, \sim (\sim T \vee W) \rightarrow \sim R, (S \rightarrow Q) \& \sim Q \vdash P$

Chapter 3
Predicate Logic

3.1   A Formal Language for Predicate Logic

Comment. Sentential logic allows us to study the logical relations among sentences that hold because of their structure, insofar as that structure is determined by the presence of connectives. But sentential logic cannot handle the similarity between 'Kareem is tall' and 'Akeem is tall', not to mention 'Someone is tall'—these would be represented as P, Q, and R, as if they had nothing in common. We now introduce a new language that accommodates this further structure.

vocabulary

Definition. The **VOCABULARY OF PREDICATE LOGIC** consists of
- **SENTENCE LETTERS,**
- **CONNECTIVES,**
- **NAMES,**
- **VARIABLES,**
- **PREDICATE LETTERS,**
- the **IDENTITY SYMBOL,**
- **QUANTIFIERS,** and
- **PARENTHESES.**

Sentence letters, connectives, and parentheses are adopted from the language of sentential logic.

names

Definition. A **NAME** is a symbol from the following list:

$$a, b, c, d, a_1, b_1, c_1, d_1, a_2, b_2, \ldots.$$

variables

Definition. A **VARIABLE** is a symbol from the following list:

$$u, v, w, x, y, z, u_1, v_1, w_1, x_1, y_1, z_1, u_2, \ldots.$$

Comment. Names and variables are used to refer to objects in much the same way as names and certain kinds of pronouns in English. Section 3.2 deals with translation between English and the language defined in this section.

Comment. Where there is no possibility of confusion we shall sometimes use lowercase letters other than those listed above as names.

1-place predicate letter

Definition. A **1-PLACE PREDICATE LETTER** is any symbol from the following list:

$$A^1, \ldots, Z^1, A^1_0, \ldots, Z^1_0, \ldots.$$

2-place

A **2-PLACE PREDICATE LETTER** is any symbol from the following list:

$$A^2, \ldots, Z^2, A^2_0, \ldots, Z^2_0, \ldots$$

n-place

In general, an *n*-**PLACE PREDICATE LETTER** is any symbol from the list

$$A^n, \ldots, Z^n, A^n_0, \ldots, Z^n_0, \ldots$$

many-place   *Comment.* Predicate letters with more than one place are referred to as **MANY-PLACE PREDICATE LETTERS.** Predicate letters will sometimes be referred to as 'predicates' for short.

Comment. In practice the superscripts can and will be omitted. Any of the capital letters may appear as sentence letters or predicate letters. It is usually possible to tell how a letter is being used in a wff by looking at the number of names or variables immediately following it. A capital letter with no names or variables is a sentence letter, one followed by one name or variable is a 1-place predicate, and so on. Also, the letters 'R' and 'S' are sometimes reserved for 2-place predicates.

identity   *Definition.* The symbol '=' is the **IDENTITY SYM-**
symbol   **BOL.**

Comment. The identity symbol is used to represent the relationship of numerical identity, such as, for example, that Mark Twain is identical to (i.e., one and the same as) Samuel Langhorne Clemens.

metavariables *Comment.* The Greek letters α, β, γ, etc. are used as **METAVARIABLES** for the names and variables of predicate logic.

universal
quantifier

Definition. A **UNIVERSAL QUANTIFIER** is any symbol of the form

$$\forall \alpha$$

where α is a variable.

Comment. Universal quantifiers correspond to the English word 'every'.

existential
quantifier

Definition. An **EXISTENTIAL QUANTIFIER** is any symbol of the form

$$\exists \alpha$$

where α is a variable.

Comment. Existential quantifiers correspond to the English word 'some'.

expression

Definition. An **EXPRESSION OF PREDICATE LOGIC** is any sequence of items from the vocabulary of predicate logic.

wffs

Definition. A **WELL-FORMED FORMULA** of predicate logic is any expression in accordance with the following seven rules:

(1) Sentence letters are wffs.

(2) An *n*-place predicate letter followed by *n* names is a wff.

(3) Expressions of the form $\alpha=\beta$ where α and β are names are wffs.

Comment. Although the placement of the identity symbol superficially resembles that of a connective, it is in fact a special two-place predicate. For historical reasons alone it is placed between α and β rather than in front of them.

atomic sentence

[*Definition.* Wffs of the form specified in rules 1–3 are the **ATOMIC SENTENCES** of predicate logic. Those conforming to rule 3 are also known as **IDENTITY STATEMENTS**.]

Comment. We adopt the practice of omitting superscripts from predicate letters.

(4) Negations, conjunctions, disjunctions, conditionals, and biconditionals of wffs are wffs.

Comment. The formation rules of chapter 1 are subsumed by this clause.

(5) If ϕ is a wff, then the result of replacing at least one occurrence of a name in ϕ by a new variable α (i.e., α not in ϕ) and prefixing $\forall\alpha$ is a wff.

universal wff

[*Definition.* Such wffs are called **UNIVERSALLY QUANTIFIED** wffs, or **UNIVERSAL** wffs.]

(6) **If ϕ is a wff, then the result of replacing at least one occurrence of a name in ϕ by a new variable α (i.e., α not in ϕ) and prefixing ∃α is a wff.**

existential wff [*Definition*. Such wffs are called **EXISTENTIALLY QUANTIFIED** wffs, or **EXISTENTIAL** wffs.]

(7) **Nothing else is a wff.**

Examples.
Wffs of this language include the following:

$((Fa \lor Fb) \rightarrow Gab)$

$\exists yFy$

$\forall x(Fx \rightarrow Gx)$

$\forall x\forall y(Rxy \rightarrow Ryx)$

$(\exists xFx \leftrightarrow \forall xGx)$

$\sim\exists x(Fx \leftrightarrow \sim\forall yGy)$

$(\exists xFx \rightarrow P)$

$\forall x\exists yFyxb$

$\sim a=b$

$\forall x \ x=x$

$\forall x\forall y(x=y \rightarrow y=x)$

Exercise 3.1.1 Which of the following expressions are wffs? If an expression is a wff, say whether it is an atomic sentence, a negation, a conditional, a conjunction, a disjunction, a biconditional, a universal, or an existential. (Note: Any wff must fall into exactly one of these categories.)

i*	Fz
ii*	∀xGac
iii*	∀xGcax
iv*	∃x∀y(Gxy & Gyx)
v*	∀x(Gxy ↔ ∃yHy)
vi*	∃x(Ax → ∀xFxx)
vii*	∀x∀y(Fxy → ∀z(Hxyz & Jz))
viii*	∀xFxx ↔ ∀x∀yFxy
ix*	~∀x~∃z(Hz ∨ Jx)
x*	Ga → ∀x~(Ha ∨ Fxx)
xi*	P → Gab
xii*	~(P & ~∃xFx)
xiii*	∀x(Fx) & P
xiv*	∃y(Fyyy & P)
xv*	∀xyz(Fzx ↔ Hxyz)
xvi*	b=b
xvii*	(a=a)
xviii*	P=c
xix*	Fa=Fa
xx*	∀z(Fz → a=b)
xxi*	∀x(x=x)
xxii*	∃x(Fx=Gx)
xxiii*	~∀x(Fx & ∃y x=y)
xxiv*	(~a=b ↔ ~∀x(Fxa & Fbx))
xxv*	∀x∃y(~x=y → y=~x)

quantifier   *Comment.* When a wff contains an uninterrupted se-
convention   quence of quantifiers of the same type, existential or
universal, it is often convenient to omit repetitions of ∃
or ∀.

Examples.
The expression
     ∀xyz(Fxy & Gyz ↔ Hzx)
will be read as shorthand for
     ∀x∀y∀z(Fxy & Gyz ↔ Hzx).

The expression
     ∃xy∀zw(Fxyz & Gwx → ~Hzx)
is to be read as
     ∃x∃y∀z∀w(Fxyz & Gwx → ~Hzx).

non-identity   We introduce the special symbol ≠ that may be used to
abbreviate statements of the form ~α = β thus: α ≠ β.
It will be useful to bear in mind that sentences of this
form are *negations*, not atomic.

Comment. As with the parenthesis-dropping conventions introduced in chapter 1, the formulas allowed by
the conventions here are not strictly well-formed. They
are merely acceptable abbreviations for wffs.

open formula   *Definition.* An **OPEN FORMULA** is the result of replacing at least one occurrence of a name in a wff by a new variable (one not already occurring in the wff).

Comment. Open formulas are not wffs and hence never appear as sentences in proofs. The notion of an open formula is used to present the rules of proof for predicate logic.

Examples.
Fx is an open formula.
It occurs as part of the wff $\forall$xFx.

Fxy is an open formula.
It occurs as part of the open formula $\exists$yFxy, which in turn is part of the wff $\forall$x$\exists$yFxy.

scope   *Definition.* The **SCOPE** of a quantifier in a given formula is the shortest open formula to the right of the quantifier.

Examples.
In the wff
$$(\forall xFx \ \& \ \exists y(Fy \rightarrow Gy)),$$
the scope of $\forall$x is the expression
$$Fx$$
and the scope of $\exists$y is the expression
$$(Fy \rightarrow Gy).$$

In the wff
$$\exists y(Fy \& \forall z(Gz \lor {\sim}Rzy)),$$
the scope of $\exists y$ is
$$(Fy \& \forall z(Gz \lor {\sim}Rzy)),$$
but the scope of $\forall z$ is
$$(Gz \lor {\sim}Rzy).$$

wider and narrower scope

Definition. A quantifier whose scope contains another other quantifier is said to have **WIDER SCOPE** than the second. The second is said to have **NARROWER SCOPE** than the first.

bound variable

Definition. A variable, α, that is in the scope of a quantifier for that variable (i.e. $\forall \alpha$ or $\exists \alpha$) is called a **BOUND VARIABLE**. A variable that is not bound by a quantifier is said to be **UNBOUND** or **FREE**.

Exercise 3.1.2* Identify all the open formulas appearing in exercise 3.1. If an open formula appears in an expression that is not well-formed, give an example of a wff in which it might appear.

Exercise 3.1.3 In the following sentences, determine the scopes of all quantifiers.

i $\forall x(Px \rightarrow \forall zRxz)$
ii ${\sim}\forall xPx \leftrightarrow \forall x\forall zRxz$

iii $\forall xPx \rightarrow \forall z{\sim}\forall xRxz$

iv $\forall z(Px \rightarrow \forall xRxz)$

v $\forall x\exists yFyxb$

vi $\exists y(Fy \,\&\, \forall z(Gz \lor {\sim}Rzy))$

vii $\forall x\forall y(Fxy \rightarrow \forall z(Hxyz \,\&\, Jz))$

viii $\forall x\forall y(Rxy \rightarrow Ryx)$

ix $\exists z\exists x(Fxz \rightarrow \forall yGyxa)$

x $\exists x(x{=}a \rightarrow \forall yGyaa)$

3.2   **Translation of English to Quantified Wffs**

translation scheme

Definition. A translation scheme for the language of predicate logic consists of a pairing of predicate letters with English predicate phrases and of names of predicate logic with names in English. We also include metavariables with the predicates and associated phrases to indicate the appropriate order for names and variables.

Example.
According to the translation scheme

    $L\alpha\beta$: α likes β

    a: Abigail,

the sentence

    'Abigail likes everything'

is translated as

    $\forall xLax$.

Comment. It is possible to give several non-equivalent translation schemes for sentences of English, depending on how many places are assigned to the predicates.

Example.
Using the translation scheme

     Fα: α is the father of Mary

     a: John,

F is specified as a 1-place predicate. Using this scheme, the sentence

     John is Mary's father

is translated as

     Fa.

Using the translation scheme

     Fαβ: α is the father of β

     a: John

     b: Mary,

F is specified as a 2-place predicate with the first position (occupied by α) corresponding to the subject of the phrase 'is the father of' and the second (occupied by β) corresponding to its object. Using this scheme, the sentence

     John is Mary's father

is translated as

     Fab.

Comment. The choice of whether to represent English phrases with one-place or many-place predicates is dependent on the degree of structure that must be included in order for an argument to be analyzed adequately. In general, more detail is better than less detail, since arguments may be labeled invalid erroneously if insufficient detail is represented.

Comment. The logical forms of many English sentences can be captured with the quantifiers introduced in section 3.1. The following is an incomplete list of some of the more common sentences.

universals   Variants whose logical form is
              ∀xFx
          include the following:
              Everything is F.
              All things are F.

          Variants whose logical form is
              ∀x(Fx → Gx)
          include the following:
              Every F is a G.
              All Fs are Gs.
              If it's an F, it's a G.
              Everything that is F is G.
              Anything that is an F is a G.
              Any F is G.
              If something is an F, it is a G.
              Only Gs are Fs.

There are several variants having the form
$$\forall x(Fx \rightarrow \sim Gx)$$
including these:

No Fs are Gs.

Not a single F is G.

Fs are never Gs.

Every F is not G.

existentials   Variants with the form
$$\exists x Fx$$
include the following:

Something is F.

There exists an F.

There is at least one F.

Variants having the form
$$\exists x(Fx \ \& \ Gx)$$
include the following:

Some Fs are Gs.

At least one F is G.

There exists an F that is G.

Comment. Notice the difference between translating 'Every F is G' (equivalently 'All Fs are Gs') and 'Some Fs are G'. In the first case, an arrow is used in the scope of a universal quantifier. In the second, an ampersand is the appropriate connective in the scope of the existential quantifier.

Comment. When translating sentences of English without the use of the identity symbol, the distinction between 'Some F is G' ('At least one F is G') and 'Some Fs are G' ('At least two Fs are G') cannot be represented. We comment on the translation of 'at least *n*' below.

identity Variants with the form

$$\alpha = \beta$$

include the following:

α is β.

α is (numerically) identical to β.

α is the same (entity) as β.

α and β are one and the same.

α is the very same individual as β.

quantities Numerical quantities can be expressed using the quantifiers in conjunction with the identity symbol.

at least *n* The existential quantifier expresses 'at least one'. Other numerical quantities can be expressed by asserting the existence of non-identical objects. Thus, for example:

$\exists xy \; x \neq y$ At least two

$\exists xyz((x \neq y \;\&\; x \neq z) \;\&\; y \neq z)$ At least three

The sentence 'There are at least two dogs' may be translated $\exists x \exists y((Dx \;\&\; Dy) \;\&\; x \neq y)$.

exactly *n*   There are exactly *n* objects if there are at least *n*, and all objects are identical to one or other of those *n*. For example:

$\exists x \forall y\ x=y$ Exactly one

$\exists xy(x \neq y\ \&\ \forall z(z=x \lor z=y))$ Exactly two

$\exists xyz(((x \neq y\ \&\ x \neq z)\ \&\ y \neq z)$

$\&\ \forall w((w=x \lor w=y) \lor w=z))$ Exactly three

at most *n*   There are at most *n* objects if there are exactly zero, or exactly one, etc., up to exactly *n* objects. For example, 'There are at most two dogs' may be translated as:

$\sim\exists x Dx \lor (\exists x(Dx\ \&\ \forall y(Dy \rightarrow y=x)) \lor$

$\exists xy(((Dx\ \&\ Dy)\ \&\ x \neq y)\ \&\ \forall z(Dz \rightarrow z=x \lor z=y))$

This is equivalent to saying that there are not three distinct dogs, i.e.:

$\sim\exists xyz((Dx\ \&\ (Dy\ \&\ Dz))\ \&\ (x \neq y\ \&\ (x \neq z\ \&\ y \neq z)))$

Comment. There are many subtleties in the translation of English quantifier phrases into the language of predicate logic. Such phrases often introduce ambiguity into the expressions of English. The exercises below illustrate some of the subtleties and ambiguities.

Exercise 3.2   Give translation schemes and translate the following sentences of English into the language of predicate logic. If a sentence is ambiguous, give all the reasonable translations of it.

(1–22: Translate using one-place predicates only.)

1*	All dogs are mammals.
2*	Some sharks are ovoviviparous.
3*	No fishes are endothermic.
4*	Not all fishes are pelagic.
5*	Reptiles and amphibians are not endothermic.
6*	Some primates and rodents are arboreal.
7*	Only lagomorphs gnaw.
8*	Among spiders, only tarantulas and black widows are poisonous.
9*	All and only marsupials have pouches.
10*	No fish have wings unless they belong to the family *Exocoetidae.*
11*	Some organisms are chordates and some organisms are molluscs, but nothing is both a chordate and a mollusc.
12*	None but phylogenists are intelligent.
13*	Animals behave normally if not watched.
14*	Animals behave normally only if not watched.
15*	Some sharks are pelagic fish, but not all pelagic fish are sharks.
16*	If Shamu is a whale and all whales are mammals, then Shamu is a mammal.
17*	No sparrow builds a nest unless it has a mate.
18*	No organism that is edentulous is a predator.
19*	All predators are not herbivorous.
20*	Not all predators are carnivorous.

21*   A mammal with wings is a bat.

22*   A mammal with wings is flying.

(23–29: Try these first with one-place predicates, then with many-place predicates.)

23*   Shamu can do every trick.

24*   Shamu can do any trick.

25*   Shamu cannot do every trick.

26*   Shamu cannot do any trick.

27*   If any whale can do a trick, Shamu can.

28*   If every whale can do a trick, Shamu can.

29*   If any whale can do a trick, any whale can do a trick.

(30–57: Translations with many-place predicates.)

30*   Godzilla ate Bambi.

31*   Something ate Bambi.

32*   Godzilla ate something.

33*   Bambi ate everything.

34*   Everything ate Bambi.

35*   Something ate something.

36*   Something ate everything.

37*   Everything ate something.

38*   Everything ate everything.

39*   Everything ate itself.

40*   Something ate itself.

41*   Nothing ate itself.

42*   Something ate nothing.

43*   Everyone said something to everyone.

44*   Everyone said something to someone.

45*   Everyone said nothing to someone.

46*   No one said anything to anyone.

47*   There is a reptile smaller than a cat but larger than a dog.

48*	Some fishes swim slower than humans.
49*	Some fishes are smaller than every mammal.
50*	Some whales eat only fast-moving fishes.
51*	Some whales do not eat any fast-moving fishes.
52*	If anything eats fast-moving fishes, sharks do.
53*	Jaguars' tails are longer than ocelots' tails.
54*	If an organism is symbiotic with a clown fish then it is a sea anemone.
55*	The phalanges of birds are homologous to the phalanges of humans whereas the eyes of octopi are analogous but not homologous to the eyes of mammals and birds.
56*	Some whales eat more than all fishes.
57*	There is a monkey who grooms all and only those monkeys who do not groom themselves.

(Translations involving the identity symbol.)

58*	Exactly one cheetah exists.
59*	There is only one Paris.
60*	Bambi ate at least two trees.
61*	Bambi ate everything except himself.
62*	Every dog has exactly one tail.
63	Godzilla ate Bambi, and something else ate Godzilla.
64	Bambi was not eaten by Godzilla but by something else.
65	Godzilla ate nothing but Bambi.
66	Godzilla ate everything except Bambi.
67	Only Bambi is afraid of Godzilla.
68	Nothing but Godzilla likes Bambi.
69	There is a fish that's bigger than all the others.
70	Nobody likes somebody who eats everything except Bambi.

3.3   Primitive Rules of Proof

Comment. We introduce six new primitive rules of proof: universal elimination, universal introduction, existential introduction, existential elimination, identity introduction, and identity elimination. To allow succinct statements of the first four of these, the notions of universalization, existentialization, and instance are defined.

universalization   *Definition.* A **UNIVERSALIZATION** of a sentence with respect to a given name occurring in the sentence is obtained by the following two steps:

(1) Replace all occurrences of the name in the sentence by a variable α, where α does not already occur in the sentence.

(2) Prefix $\forall \alpha$ to the open formula resulting from step 1.

Examples.
Universalizations of
$$(Fa \rightarrow Ga)$$
include
$$\forall x(Fx \rightarrow Gx)$$
and $\forall y(Fy \rightarrow Gy)$.

Universalizations of
  Faa
include
  $\forall$xFxx
and $\forall$yFyy.

existentia-
lization

Definition. An **EXISTENTIALIZATION** of a sentence with respect to a given name occurring in the sentence is obtained by the following two steps:

(1) Replace at least one occurrence of the name in the sentence by a variable α, where α does not already occur in the sentence.

(2) Prefix $\exists\alpha$ to the open formula resulting from step 1.

Comment. Notice the difference between step 1 in the definition of universalization and step 1 in the definition of existentialization. Universalization requires replacement of *all* occurrences of the name by with α.

Examples.
Existentializations of
  (Fa $\rightarrow$ Ga)
include
  $\exists$x(Fx $\rightarrow$ Gx),
  $\exists$x(Fa $\rightarrow$ Gx),
and $\exists$y(Fy $\rightarrow$ Ga).

Existentializations of
    Faa
include
    ∃xFxx,
    ∃xFax,
and ∃yFya.

instance   *Definition.* An **INSTANCE** of a universally or existentially quantified sentence is the result of the following two steps:

(1) Remove the initial quantifier.

(2) In the open formula resulting from step 1, uni-
     formly replace all occurrences of the unbound
     variable by a name.

Comment. This is called **INSTANTIATING** the sentence. The name is called the **INSTANTIAL NAME**.

Examples.
The sentence
    ∀xFx
has instances
    Fa, Fb, Fc, etc.

The sentence
    ∃x(Fx & Gx)
has instances
    (Fa & Ga), (Fb & Gb), (Fc & Gc), etc.

The sentence
$$\exists x \forall y(Fxy \rightarrow Gy)$$
has instances
$$\forall y(Fay \rightarrow Gy), \ \forall y(Fby \rightarrow Gy), \text{ etc.}$$

Exercise 3.3.1* Pair wffs and their instances from the list of sentences below. Some formulas may appear in several pairs. Others may appear in none.

i	$\forall x Fax$
ii	$\exists x(Fxa \ \& \ \forall y Gyxa)$
iii	$\exists x Fax$
iv	Fab
v	$\exists y \lor x Fyx$
vi	$\exists zx(Fxz \ \& \ \forall y Gyxa)$
vii	$\forall xy Fxy$
viii	$\forall x Fxa$
ix	$\exists zx(Fxz \ \& \ \forall y Gyxz)$
x	$Fba \ \& \ \forall y Gyba$

Comment. The primitive rules of proof for predicate logic include all the primitive rules from chapter 1. There are also introduction and elimination rules for the two quantifiers and for the identity symbol. Two of the new rules have conditions that must be met for the application of the rules to be correct.

universal-elim Given a universally quantified sentence (at line m), conclude any instance of it.

Condition:	None.
Annotation:	$m \ \forall \mathbf{E}$
Assumption set:	same as line m.
Also known as:	Universal Instantiation.

Examples.

(a)

1	(1)	$\forall x Fx$	A
1	(2)	Fa	1 $\forall$E
1	(3)	Fb	1 $\forall$E

(b)

1	(1)	$\forall y Ryy$	A
1	(2)	Rbb	1 $\forall$E

universal-intro Given a sentence (at line m) containing at least one occurrence of a name, conclude a universalization of the sentence with respect to that name.

Condition:	The name in question must not occur in any assumptions in m's assumption set.
Annotation:	$m \ \forall \mathbf{I}$
Assumption-set:	same as line m.
Also known as:	Universal Generalization.

Examples.

(a)

1	(1)	$\forall xFx$	A
1	(2)	Fb	1 $\forall$E
1	(3)	$\forall xFx$	2 $\forall$I
1	(4)	$\forall yFy$	2 $\forall$I

(b)

1	(1)	$\forall x(Fx \rightarrow Gx)$	A
1	(2)	$Fa \rightarrow Ga$	1 $\forall$E
3	(3)	$\forall xFx$	A
3	(4)	Fa	3 $\forall$E
1,3	(5)	Ga	2,4 $\rightarrow$E
1,3	(6)	$\forall xGx$	5 $\forall$I

Example of violation of the $\forall$I condition.

(c)

1	(1)	$\forall x(Fx \rightarrow Gx)$	A
2	(2)	Fa	A
1	(3)	$Fa \rightarrow Ga$	1 $\forall$E
1,2	(4)	Ga	2,3 $\rightarrow$E
wrong! 1,2	(5)	$\forall xGx$	4 $\forall$I

Comment. Ordinarily we cannot conclude $\forall xFx$ merely from Fa—the fact that one thing is F doesn't guarantee that everything is F! The condition on $\forall$I ensures that we do not make this mistake. If the sentence Fa is true, and furthermore *would still be true no matter what the name denotes*, then clearly everything is F, so we can conclude $\forall xFx$. When the condition on $\forall$I is met, then we are in such a situation: if we prove Fa from assumptions that do not contain the name a and hence say nothing in particular about its referent, then we could just as well have used a different name, say b, and proved Fb. In fact, when the condition on ∀I is met, any proof of Fa can be turned into a proof of Fb just by replacing any involved occurrences of the name a by the name b. This is sufficient to guarantee that everything is F; hence, we can conclude ∀xFx.

existential-intro

Given a sentence (at line *m*) containing at least one occurrence of a name, conclude an existentialization of that sentence with respect to that name.

Condition: None.
Annotation: **m ∃I**
Assumption-set: same as line *m*.
Also known as: Existential Generalization.

Examples.

(a)

1	(1)	Fa	A
1	(2)	∃xFx	1 ∃I

(b)

1	(1)	∀x(Fx → Gx)	A
2	(2)	Fa	A
1	(3)	Fa → Ga	1 ∀E
1,2	(4)	Ga	2,3 →E
1,2	(5)	Fa & Ga	2,4 &I
1,2	(6)	∃x(Fx & Gx)	5 ∃I

(c)

| 1 | (1) | $\forall x Fax$ | A |
| 1 | (2) | $\exists y \forall x Fyx$ | 1 $\exists$I |

existential-elim

Given a sentence (at line m) and an assumption (at line i) that is an instance of some existentially quantified sentence that is present (at line k), conclude the given sentence again.

Condition: The instantial name at line i must not appear in the sentence at line k or in the sentence at line m. Also, it must not appear in any of the assumptions belonging to the assumption set at line m, other than the instance i itself.

Annotation: k,m $\exists$**E** (i)

Assumption set: all assumptions at line m other than i, and all assumptions at line k.

Examples.

(a)

1	(1)	$\exists x Fx$	A
2	(2)	Fa	A
2	(3)	$Fa \lor Ga$	2 $\lor$I
2	(4)	$\exists x(Fx \lor Gx)$	3 $\exists$I
1	(5)	$\exists x(Fx \lor Gx)$	1,4 $\exists$E (2)

(b)

1	(1)	∃x(Fxx → P)	A
2	(2)	Faa → P	A
3	(3)	∀xFxx	A
3	(4)	Faa	3 ∀E
2,3	(5)	P	2,4 →E
1,3	(6)	P	1,5 ∃E (2)

Examples of violation of ∃E condition.

(a)

1	(1)	∃xFx	A
2	(2)	Fa	A
3	(3)	Ga	A
2,3	(4)	Fa & Ga	2,3 &I
2,3	(5)	∃x(Fx & Gx)	4 ∃I
wrong! 1,3	(6)	∃x(Fx & Gx)	1,5 ∃E (2)

(b)

1	(1)	∃xFx	A
2	(2)	Fa	A
wrong! 1	(3)	Fa	1,2 ∃E (2)

(c)

1	(1)	∃xFax	A
2	(2)	Faa	A
2	(3)	∃xFxx	2 ∃I
wrong! 1	(4)	∃xFxx	1,3 ∃E (2)

Comment. If all we know is that *something* is F, we are not entitled to reason as if we know *what* it is that is F. As in the case of ∀I, a use of ∃E that meets the conditions above and uses a certain instantial name can be turned into a proof of the same conclusion from the same assumptions but using any different instantial name. This shows that the conclusion does not rest on any assumptions about the actual identity of the thing that is said to exist. That is, if we apply ∃E to ∃xFx by discharging the assumed instance Fa, the conditions ensure that we do not mistakenly use any information about the referent of 'a' *in particular.* After all, ∃xFx says only that something is F—it doesn't tell us *which* individual is F.

identity-intro   Conclude any sentence of the form $\alpha=\alpha$.

Condition: None.
Annotation: **=I**
Assumption set: Empty.

Example.

(1)   c=c   =I

Comment. An identity statement of the form $\alpha=\alpha$, like a theorem, requires no assumptions to justify its assertion.

identity-elim Given a sentence ϕ (at line *m*) containing a name α, and another sentence (at line *n*) that is an identity statement containing α and another name β, conclude a sentence that is the result of replacing at least one occurrence of α in ϕ with β.

Condition:	None.
Annotation:	**m,n =E**
Assumption set:	The union of the assumption sets at lines *m* and *n*.
Also known as:	Leibniz's Law, Substitutivity of Identity

Examples.

(a)

1	(1)	Fa	A
2	(2)	a=b	A
1,2	(3)	Fb	1,2 =E

(b)

1	(1)	Fa & Ga	A
2	(2)	b=a	A
1,2	(3)	Fb & Ga	1,2 =E
1,2	(4)	Fb & Gb	1,2 =E

(c)

1	(1)	∀x(Fxa → x=a)	A
2	(2)	Fba	A
1	(3)	Fba → b=a	1 ∀E
1,2	(4)	b=a	2,3→E
1,2	(5)	∀x(Fxb → x=b)	1,4 =E

Comment. The rule of identity elimination is not regarded as valid in all contexts. For instance, if Frank believes that Mark Twain is a novelist then, even though Twain=Clemens, it does not follow that he believes Samuel Langhorne Clemens is a novelist (if, for example, he has heard the name "Twain" but never "Clemens"). For historical reasons, contexts where the rule fails, such as belief reports, are called *intensional* contexts in contrast to the *extensional* contexts provided by the ordinary predicates which the language developed in this chapter is intended to represent.

Exercise 3.3.2 Prove the following sequents, using the primitive rules of predicate logic. You may also use derived sentential rules.

S87*	$\exists x(Gx \mathbin{\&} {\sim}Fx), \forall x(Gx \to Hx) \vdash \exists x(Hx \mathbin{\&} {\sim}Fx)$
S88*	$\exists x(Gx \mathbin{\&} \Gamma x), \forall x(Fx \to {\sim}Hx) \vdash \exists x{\sim}Hx$
S89*	$\forall x(Gx \to {\sim}Fx), \forall x({\sim}Fx \to {\sim}Hx) \vdash \forall x(Gx \to {\sim}Hx)$
S90	$\exists x(Fx \mathbin{\&} Ga), \forall x(Fx \to Hx) \vdash Ga \mathbin{\&} \exists x(Fx \mathbin{\&} Hx)$
S91*	$\forall x(Gx \to \exists y(Fy \mathbin{\&} Hy)) \vdash \forall x{\sim}Fx \to {\sim}\exists zGz$
S92*	$\forall x(Gx \to Hx \mathbin{\&} Jx), \forall x(Fx \vee {\sim}Jx \to Gx) \vdash \forall x(Fx \to Hx)$
S93*	$\forall x(Gx \mathbin{\&} Kx \leftrightarrow Hx), {\sim}\exists x(Fx \mathbin{\&} Gx) \vdash \forall x{\sim}(Fx \mathbin{\&} Hx)$
S94	$\forall x(Gx \to Hx), \exists x((Fx \mathbin{\&} Gx) \mathbin{\&} Mx) \vdash \exists x(Fx \mathbin{\&} (Hx \mathbin{\&} Mx))$
S95*	$\forall x({\sim}Gx \vee {\sim}Hx), \forall x((Jx \to Fx) \to Hx) \vdash {\sim}\exists x(Fx \mathbin{\&} Gx)$
S96*	${\sim}\exists x({\sim}Gx \mathbin{\&} Hx), \forall x(Fx \to {\sim}Hx) \vdash \forall x(Fx \vee {\sim}Gx \to {\sim}Hx)$
S97	$\forall x{\sim}(Gx \mathbin{\&} Hx), \exists x(Fx \mathbin{\&} Gx) \vdash \exists x(Fx \mathbin{\&} {\sim}Hx)$
S98	$\exists x(Fx \mathbin{\&} {\sim}Hx), {\sim}\exists x(Fx \mathbin{\&} {\sim}Gx) \vdash {\sim}\forall x(Gx \to Hx)$
S99	$\forall x(Hx \to Hx \mathbin{\&} Gx), \exists x({\sim}Gx \mathbin{\&} Fx) \vdash \exists x(Fx \mathbin{\&} {\sim}Hx)$
S100	$\forall x(Hx \to {\sim}Gx), {\sim}\exists x(Fx \mathbin{\&} {\sim}Gx) \vdash \forall x{\sim}(Fx \mathbin{\&} Hx)$
S101*	$\forall x(Fx \leftrightarrow Gx) \vdash \forall xFx \leftrightarrow \forall xGx$
S102*	$\exists x\,Fx \to \forall y(Gy \to Hy), \exists xJx \to \exists xGx \vdash \exists x(Fx \mathbin{\&} Jx) \to \exists zHz$
S103	$\exists xFx \vee \exists xGx, \forall x(Fx \to Gx) \vdash \exists xGx$

S104 $\forall x(Fx \rightarrow \sim Gx) \vdash \sim \exists x(Fx \& Gx)$

S105* $\forall x(Fx \vee Hx \rightarrow Gx \& Kx), \sim\forall x(Kx \& Gx) \vdash \exists x\sim Hx$

S106 $\forall x(Fx \& Gx \rightarrow Hx), Ga \& \forall xFx \vdash Fa \& Ha$

S107* $\forall x(Fx \leftrightarrow \forall yGy) \vdash \forall xFx \vee \forall x\sim Fx$

S108 $\forall y(Fa \rightarrow (\exists xGx \rightarrow Gy)), \forall x(Gx \rightarrow Hx), \forall x(\sim Jx \rightarrow \sim Hx)$
            $\vdash \exists x\sim Jx \rightarrow \sim Fa \vee \forall x\sim Gx$

S109* $\forall x(Dx \rightarrow Fx) \vdash \forall z(Dz \rightarrow (\forall y(Fy \rightarrow Gy) \rightarrow Gz))$

S110 $\exists xFx \leftrightarrow \forall y(Fy \vee Gy \rightarrow Hy), \exists xHx, \sim\forall z\sim Fz \vdash \exists x(Fx \& Hx)$

S111* $\forall xFx \vdash \sim\exists xGx \leftrightarrow \sim(\exists x(Fx \& Gx) \& \forall y(Gy \rightarrow Fy))$

S112* $\forall x(\exists yFyx \rightarrow \forall zFxz) \vdash \forall yx(Fyx \rightarrow Fxy)$

S113 $\exists x(Fx \& \forall yGxy), \forall xy(Gxy \rightarrow Gyx) \vdash \exists x(Fx \& \forall yGyx)$

S114 $\exists x\sim\forall y(Gxy \rightarrow Gyx) \vdash \exists x\exists y(Gxy \& \sim Gyx)$

S115 $\forall x(Gx \rightarrow \forall y(Fy \rightarrow Hxy)), \exists x(Fx \& \forall z\sim Hxz) \vdash \sim\forall xGx$

S116 $\forall xy(Fxy \rightarrow Gxy) \vdash \forall x(Fxx \rightarrow \exists y(Gxy \& Fyx))$

S117* $\forall xy(Fxy \rightarrow \sim Fyx) \vdash \sim\exists xFxx$

S118 $\forall x\exists y(Fxy \& \sim Fyx) \vdash \exists x\sim\forall yFxy$

S119 $\forall y(\exists x\sim Fxy \rightarrow \sim Fyy) \vdash \forall x(Fxx \rightarrow \forall yFyx)$

S120 $\exists xFxx \rightarrow \forall xyFxy \vdash \forall x(Fxx \rightarrow \forall yFxy)$

S121 $a=b \vdash b=a$

S122 $a=b \& b=c \vdash a=c$

S123* $a=b, b\neq c \vdash a\neq c$

S124 $Fa \& \forall x(Fx \rightarrow x=a), \exists x(Fx \& Gx) \vdash Ga$

S125* $\forall x\ x=x \rightarrow \exists xFx, \forall x(\sim Fx \vee Gx) \vdash \exists x(Fx \& Gx)$

S126 $\forall x(Fx \rightarrow Gx), \forall x(Gx \rightarrow Hx), Fa \& \sim Hb \vdash a\neq b$

S127* $\exists x((Fx \& \forall y(Fy \rightarrow y=x)) \& Gx), \sim Ga \vdash \sim Fa$

S128 $\exists x\forall y((\sim Fxy \rightarrow x=y) \& Gx) \vdash \forall x(\sim Gx \rightarrow \exists y(y\neq x \& Fyx))$

S129 $\exists x(Px \& (\forall y(Py \rightarrow y=x) \& Qx)), \exists x\sim(\sim Px \vee \sim Fx)$
            $\vdash \exists x(Fx \& Qx)$

S130* $\forall x\exists yGyx, \forall xy(Gxy \rightarrow \sim Gyx) \vdash \sim\exists y\forall x(x\neq y \rightarrow Gyx)$

3.4   Sequents, Theorems, and Derived Rules of Proof

Exercise 3.4.1 Prove the following sequents, using the primitive rules from chapter 3 and any of the primitive or derived rules from chapter 1.

S150*	$\sim\forall xPx \dashv\vdash \exists x\sim Px$	**Quantifier Exchange**
S151	$\sim\exists xPx \dashv\vdash \forall x\sim Px$	QE
S152	$\sim\forall x\sim Px \dashv\vdash \exists xPx$	QE
S153	$\sim\exists x\sim Px \dashv\vdash \forall xPx$	QE
S154	$\forall x(Px \mathbin{\&} Qx) \dashv\vdash \forall xPx \mathbin{\&} \forall xQx$	**Conf**inement
S155*	$\forall x(Px \rightarrow Q) \dashv\vdash \exists xPx \rightarrow Q$	Conf
S156*	$\forall xPx \lor \forall xQx \vdash \forall x(Px \lor Qx)$	Conf
S157*	$\exists xy(Px \mathbin{\&} Qy) \dashv\vdash \exists xPx \mathbin{\&} \exists xQx$	Conf
S158	$\exists x(Px \lor Qx) \dashv\vdash \exists xPx \lor \exists xQx$	Conf
S159	$\exists x(Px \rightarrow Q) \dashv\vdash \forall xPx \rightarrow Q$	Conf
S160*	$P \rightarrow \exists xQx \dashv\vdash \exists x(P \rightarrow Qx)$	Conf
S161	$P \rightarrow \forall xQx \dashv\vdash \forall x(P \rightarrow Qx)$	Conf

QE
(derived rule)

Comment. The important quantificr-cxchange rules establish that an initial tilde can always be moved to the right of an adjacent quantifier, changing the quantifier from a universal to an existential (or vice versa). Also, a tilde that immediately follows an initial quantifier can be moved to the front of the sentence provided, again, that the quantifier is changed as just described. Although the above versions of the rules (S150–S153) involve quantifications of a simple formula, it is easily recognizable that the proofs of these sequents do not depend on the simplicity of the quantified formula. **QUANTIFIER EXCHANGE (QE)** may thus be used as a derived rule of proof as below.

Example.

1	(1)	$\exists x \sim(Fx\ \&\ Gx)$	A
2	(2)	$\exists xGx \rightarrow \forall x(Fx\ \&\ Gx)$	A
1	(3)	$\sim\forall x(Fx\ \&\ Gx)$	1 QE
1,2	(4)	$\sim\exists xGx$	2,3 MTT
1,2	(5)	$\forall x\sim Gx$	4 QE

Exercise 3.4.2 Prove the following sequents, using any of the primitive or derived rules established so far.

T40	$\vdash \forall x(Fx \rightarrow Gx) \rightarrow (\forall xFx \rightarrow \forall xGx)$
T41	$\vdash \forall x(Fx \rightarrow Gx) \rightarrow (\exists xFx \rightarrow \exists xGx)$
T42	$\vdash \exists x(Fx \vee Gx) \leftrightarrow \exists xFx \vee \exists xGx$
T43	$\vdash \forall x(Fx\ \&\ Gx) \leftrightarrow \forall xFx\ \&\ \forall xGx$
T44	$\vdash \exists x(Fx\ \&\ Gx) \rightarrow \exists xFx\ \&\ \exists xGx$
T45	$\vdash \forall xFx \vee \forall xGx \rightarrow \forall x(Fx \vee Gx)$
T46	$\vdash (\exists xFx \rightarrow \exists xGx) \rightarrow \exists x(Fx \rightarrow Gx)$
T47	$\vdash (\forall xFx \rightarrow \forall xGx) \rightarrow \exists x(Fx \rightarrow Gx)$
T48	$\vdash \sim\forall x(Fx \leftrightarrow Gx) \vee (\forall xFx \leftrightarrow \forall xGx)$
T49	$\vdash \sim\forall x(Fx \leftrightarrow Gx) \vee (\exists xFx \leftrightarrow \exists xGx)$
T50	$\vdash \sim\forall x(P\ \&\ Fx) \leftrightarrow (P \rightarrow \sim\forall xFx)$
T51	$\vdash \sim\exists x(P\ \&\ Fx) \leftrightarrow (P \rightarrow \sim\exists xFx)$
T52	$\vdash \forall x(P \vee Fx) \leftrightarrow (\sim P \rightarrow \forall xFx)$
T53	$\vdash \exists x(P \vee Fx) \leftrightarrow (\sim P \rightarrow \exists xFx)$
T54	$\vdash \forall x(Fx \rightarrow P) \leftrightarrow (\exists xFx \rightarrow P)$
T55	$\vdash \sim\exists x(Fx \rightarrow P) \leftrightarrow \sim(\forall xFx \rightarrow P)$

T56   ⊢ ∀x(Fx ↔ P) → (∀xFx ↔ P)

T57   ⊢ ∀x(Fx ↔ P) → (∃xFx ↔ P)

T58   ⊢ (∃xFx ↔ P) → ∃x(Fx ↔ P)

T59*   ⊢ (∀xFx ↔ P) → ∃x(Fx ↔ P)

T60   ⊢ ∀x∃y x=y

T61   ⊢ ∀x(Fx ↔ ∃y(x=y & Fy))

T62   ⊢ ∀x(Fx ↔ ∀y(x=y → Fy))

T63   ⊢ ∀xy(Rxy ↔ x=y) → ∀xRxx

prenex form   *Comment.* The quantifier-exchange rules and the confinement rules (S154–S151) indicate that any sentence may be converted into an equivalent sentence in which no connective is outside the scope of any quantifier in the formula. Such a sentence, called a **PRENEX** sentence, has all its quantifiers in a row at the beginning of the sentence.

Exercise 3.4.3   For each of the following, find a prenex equivalent and prove the equivalence.

1*   ∀x(Px → ∀zRxz)

2*   ∃y(Fy&∀z(Hyz & Jz))

3*   ∃xFxa → ∀yGyaa

4*   ~∀xFx → ∃xHx

5*   ~∃x(∃yFyx → ~∀zGzx)

Find prenex equivalents for the other non-prenex sentences in this chapter and the next.

Chapter 4
Models

4.1 **Finite Interpretations and Expansions with One-Place Predicates without Identity**

finite *Definition.* A **FINITE INTERPRETATION** for a set
interpretation of symbolic sentences (containing one-place predicates
but no many-place predicates) consists of three
components:

universe • A finite set of objects called the **UNIVERSE** or
DOMAIN. The universe must contain at least one
object.

predicate • An **EXTENSION** for each of the predicates in
extensions the sentences. Each extension is a (possibly empty) subset of the universe containing those objects
to which the predicate applies.

truth-value • **TRUTH- VALUE SPECIFICATIONS** for the
specifications sentence letters in the sentences. Each of the
sentence letters is paired with the specification
True or with the specification False.

Comment. Such an interpretation is finite because its
universe is a finite set. In the rest of this section, we
will use 'interpretation' as shorthand for *'finite
interpretation'*.

evaluation   *Comment.* Given an interpretation for a set of sentences, it will be possible to determine truth values for the sentences in the set.

Example.
Here is a conditional sentence and an interpretation in which it can bc evaluated:

$$\forall x(Fx \lor {\sim}Gx) \rightarrow P \lor \exists x(Gx \ \& \ {\sim}Fx)$$

U: {a,b,c}
F: {a,b}
G: {b}
P is False

In this interpretation the antecedent of the sentence is true since everything in the universe is either F or not G (a and b are both F, c is not G).

The consequent of the conditional is false, since both disjuncts are false. (P is specified false. The existential wff is false because there is nothing in the extension of G that is not also in the extension of F.)

The conditional is therefore false.

Comment. The procedure for determining the truth values of sentences in an interpretation for them is given more precisely in section 4.2.

**universal
expansion**

Definition. The **EXPANSION OF A UNIVERSAL WFF** relative to a universe of *n* elements consists of *n* conjuncts, where the *n*th conjunct is an instance of the formula with the name of the *n*th element in the universe as the instantial name. (We refer to this as a **UNIVERSAL EXPANSION** for short.)

Comment. Strictly speaking, all conjunctions have exactly two conjuncts. Expressions having the form φ & ψ & ... are unproblematic, however, because of the associativity of & (S40). So, it is acceptable to use the notion of a conjunction with more than two conjuncts in the definition of a universal expansion. Likewise, because of the associativity of ∨ (S41), we use the notion of a disjunct with more than two disjuncts in the definition of an existential expansion below.

Example.
The expansion of
$$\forall x(Fx \rightarrow Gx)$$
in the universe {a} is
$$(Fa \rightarrow Ga).$$
In the universe {a,b} its expansion is
$$(Fa \rightarrow Ga) \,\&\, (Fb \rightarrow Gb).$$
In the universe {a,b,c} its expansion is
$$(Fa \rightarrow Ga) \,\&\, (Fb \rightarrow Gb) \,\&\, (Fc \rightarrow Gc),$$
and so on.

existential
expansion

Definition. The **EXPANSION OF AN EXISTEN-TIAL WFF** relative to a universe of n elements consists of n disjuncts, where the nth disjunct is an instance of the formula with the name of the nth element in the universe as the instantial name. (**EXISTENTIAL EXPANSION** for short.)

Example.
The existential
      $\exists x(Fx \ \& \ Gx)$
expands to
      $(Fa \ \& \ Ga) \lor (Fb \ \& \ Gb) \lor \ldots$
for the universe $\{a,b, \ldots\}$.

overlapping
quantifiers

Comment. In cases where quantifiers overlap, expansion may take several steps, starting with the quantifier with the widest scope and then expanding those with narrower scope. Expansion is complete when no quantifiers remain.

Example.
In the universe $\{a,b\}$
      $\forall x(Fx \rightarrow \exists y Gy)$
is first expanded to
      $(Fa \rightarrow \exists y Gy) \ \& \ (Fb \rightarrow \exists y Gy),$
then to
      $((Fa \rightarrow (Ga \lor Gb)) \ \& \ (Fb \rightarrow (Ga \lor Gb)).$

truth values of complex sentences

Comment. The truth values of complex sentences in a given interpretation are determined as follows.

quantifiers

(i) Construct the expansions of all universal and existential formulas, then assign truth values for the resulting quantifier-free sentences according to steps ii–iv below. The truth value of a quantified sentence is the truth value of its expansion.

sentence letters

(ii) Sentence letters have the truth values directly assigned to them in the interpretation.

predicates

(iii) Formulas of the form $F\alpha$, where F is a predicate and α is a name, are true if the object α is in the extension of F and false otherwise.

connectives

(iv) The truth values for the sentential connectives are determined according to the usual truth-functional rules for the connectives.

Exercise 4.1.1 Give the expansions for the following sentences

                    (a) for the universe {a}

                    (b) for the universe {a,b}

                    (c) for the universe {a,b,c}

i*	$\forall x Fx$
ii*	$\exists x Fx \,\&\, P$
iii*	$\forall x Fx \rightarrow \exists x Gx$
iv*	$\forall x (Gx \leftrightarrow P) \lor \forall x Hx$
v*	$Ha \lor \exists x Gx$
vi*	$\exists x (Fx \lor Hx)$
vii*	$\forall x Fx \leftrightarrow \exists x (Fx \,\&\, {\sim}Hx)$
viii*	${\sim}\forall x (Fx \,\&\, Gx)$
ix*	${\sim}\forall x (Fx \,\&\, {\sim}\forall y Gy)$
x*	${\sim}(\forall x Gx \leftrightarrow \exists x (Hx \,\&\, {\sim}Fx))$

Exercise 4.1.2 Say whether the sentences in exercise 4.1.1 are true in the following interpretations:

a*   U: {a}, F: {a}, G: { }, H: { },
                    P is False

b*   U: {a,b}, F: {a}, G: {a,b}, H: { },
                    P is True

c*   U: {a,b,c}, F: {a,b,c}, G: {a,b}, H: {b},
                    P is False

4.2   Finite Countermodels for Arguments with One-Place Predicates without Identity

model   *Definition.* A **MODEL** for a set of sentences is an interpretation in which all the sentences in the set are true.

countermodel *Definition.* A **COUNTERMODEL** for a given argument is a model for the premises in which the conclusion is false.

Comment. The idea behind a countermodel is the same as that behind using a truth table to demonstrate that an argument is invalid. The point is to demonstrate that it is possible for all the premises of an argument to be true and still have the conclusion turn out false. Thus, a countermodel is the predicate-logic analogue of an invalidating assignment (introduced in chapter 2).

Comment. Given an invalid sequent with one-place predicates and no many-place predicates, it is always possible to find a finite countermodel. Indeed, if the sequent contains n predicates, the universe of a countermodel need not have more than 2^n elements, and will often have fewer.

Comment. Expansions provide a convenient way of demonstrating that a given interpretation is a countermodel for an argument.

Examples.

(a)

Give a countermodel and an expansion to show this sequent invalid:

$\exists x Gx \vdash P \rightarrow \forall x Gx$

Model:

U: {a,b}

G: {a}

P is True

Expansions:

The premise $\exists x Gx$ expands to

Ga $\lor$ Gb

with these truth assignments:

T $\lor$ F

T

The conclusion P $\rightarrow$ $\forall x Gx$ expands to

P $\rightarrow$ (Ga & Gb)

with these truth assignments:

T $\rightarrow$ (T & F)

T $\rightarrow$ F

F

The premise is true and the conclusion is false in this interpretation, so the argument is invalid.

(b)

Give a countermodel and an expansion to show this sequent invalid:

$$\forall xFx \rightarrow \forall xGx \vdash Fm \rightarrow \exists xGx$$

Model:

    U: {m,a}

    F: {m}

    G: { }

Expansion:

The premise ($\forall xFx \rightarrow \forall xGx$) expands to

    Fm & Fa $\rightarrow$ Gm & Ga

    T   F F   *T*

The conclusion (Fm $\rightarrow \exists xGx$) expands to

    Fm $\rightarrow$ Gm $\vee$ Ga

    T   *F* F   F F

The conclusion is false in this interpretation and the premise is true; hence, this interpretation is a counter-example for the given sequent.

Exercise 4.2   Construct countermodels and expansions to show the following sequents invalid.

i* $\forall xFx \rightarrow \forall x\ Gx \vdash \forall x(Fx \rightarrow Gx)$

ii* $\exists xFx \rightarrow \exists xGx \vdash \forall x(Fx \rightarrow Gx)$

iii* $\exists xFx\ \&\ \exists xGx \vdash \exists x(Fx\ \&\ Gx)$

iv* $\exists x(Fx \vee Gx) \vdash \forall xFx \vee \forall xGx$

v* $\exists x(Fx \rightarrow Gx) \vdash \exists xFx \rightarrow \exists xGx$

vi* $\exists x(Fx \rightarrow Gx) \vdash \forall xFx \rightarrow \forall xGx$

vii* $\forall xFx \leftrightarrow \forall xGx \vdash \forall x(Fx \leftrightarrow Gx)$

viii* $\exists xFx \leftrightarrow \exists xGx \vdash \forall x(Fx \leftrightarrow Gx)$

ix* $\forall xFx \leftrightarrow P \vdash \forall x(Fx \leftrightarrow P)$

x* $\exists xFx \leftrightarrow P \vdash \forall x(Fx \leftrightarrow P)$

xi* $\exists x(Fx \leftrightarrow P) \vdash \exists xFx \leftrightarrow P$

xii* $\exists x(Fx \leftrightarrow P) \vdash \forall xFx \leftrightarrow P$

xiii* $\forall x(Fx \rightarrow Gx), \forall x(Gx \rightarrow Hx) \vdash \forall x(Hx \rightarrow Fx)$

xiv* $\forall x(Fx \rightarrow {\sim}Hx), \forall x(Hx \rightarrow {\sim}Gx) \vdash \exists x(Fx \ \& \ Gx)$

xv* $\exists xFx \leftrightarrow \forall xGx, {\sim}\forall x(Fx \rightarrow Hx) \vdash \exists xHx \rightarrow \exists x{\sim}Gx$

xvi* $\forall x(Gx \vee {\sim}Hx), \exists x(Gx \ \& \ Fx) \vdash \exists x{\sim}Hx$

xvii* $\forall x(Fx \ \& \ Gx \rightarrow Hx), \exists x(Fx \ \& \ Hx) \vdash \exists xGx$

xviii* $\exists xFx, \exists xGx, \exists xHx \vdash \forall x(Fx \vee Gx \rightarrow Hx)$

xix* ${\sim}\forall xFx \vdash \forall x{\sim}Fx$

xx* $\exists x(Fx \rightarrow \exists yGy) \vdash \exists xFx \rightarrow \exists yGy$

4.3   Finite Countermodels for Arguments with Many-Place Predicates without Identity

ordered pair   The notation $\langle \alpha, \beta \rangle$ denotes the **ORDERED PAIR** consisting of two objects named by α and β (α and β may be the same). So long as the two objects are different objects, the ordered pair denoted by $\langle \alpha, \beta \rangle$ is different from the pair denoted by $\langle \beta, \alpha \rangle$.

Comment. The idea behind ordered pairs is easily extended to cover orderings of more than two objects.

ordered

n-tuple

An **ORDERED n-TUPLE,** $\langle \alpha_0, \alpha_1, ..., \alpha_n \rangle$, consists of the n objects named by $\alpha_0, \alpha_1, ..., \alpha_n$.

Comment. As with ordered pairs, changing the ordering of $\alpha_0, \alpha_1, ..., \alpha_n$ usually changes the identity of the n-tuple.

n-place

extensions

Definition. The **EXTENSION OF AN n-PLACE PREDICATE** is a set of ordered n-tuples of objects from the universe.

Example.

Given a universe containing the objects a, b, and c, and a two-place predicate R, the set $\{\langle a,b \rangle, \langle c,b \rangle, \langle a,a \rangle\}$ gives a possible extension for R. In this example, the sentences Rab, Rcb, and Raa are true, while the sentences Rac, Rbc, Rba, Rca, Rbb, and Rcc are all false.

finite

interpretation

Definition. A finite interpretation for a set of sentences containing one-place and many-place predicates consists of the following:

- A finite universe, or domain.

- Extensions for all the predicates appearing in the sentences.

- Truth value specifications for the sentence letters appearing in the sentences.

Example.
Given a universe
    U: {a, b}
the expansion of the wff
    $\forall x \exists y Fxy$
is constructed by first expanding the universal quantifier (since it has wider scope) to yield
    $\exists y Fay$ & $\exists y Fby$.
Each existential is then expanded to yield
    (Faa $\vee$ Fab) & (Fba $\vee$ Fbb).

Comment. The definition of an interpretation for a set of sentences containing one-place predicates, given in section 4.1, is just a special case of the definition for many-place predicates.

countermodels *Comment.* As before, a countermodel for a given sequent is a model for the premises where the conclusion is false.

Example.
The sequent
    $\forall x \exists y Rxy \vdash \exists y \forall x Rxy$
is invalid, as shown by the following interpretation:
    U: {a, b}
    R: {⟨a, b⟩, ⟨b, a⟩}

Expansions:
Premise   (Raa $\vee$ Rab) & (Rba $\vee$ Rbb)

$$F \vee T \qquad T \vee F$$
$$T \quad \& \quad T$$
$$T$$

Conclusion   (Raa & Rab) ∨ (Rba & Rbb)
$$F \ \& \ T \qquad T \ \& \ F$$
$$F \qquad \vee \qquad F$$
$$F$$

Exercise 4.3.1 Construct countermodels for the following invalid sequents.

i*	∃xFxx ⊢ ∀xyFyx
ii*	∀y∃xFxy ⊢ ∃xFxx
iii*	∀x∃yFxy ⊢ ∃x∀yFxy
iv*	∀x∃y· Fxy, ∀x∀y(Gxy → ~Fxy) ⊢ ∀x∃y~Gxy
v*	∀x(Fx → ∃yGxy) ⊢ ∀x∀y(Fx ∨ ~Gxy)
vi*	∀x∃y∀zVxyz ⊢ ∃y∀x∀zVxyz
vii*	∀x~∀yTxy ⊢ ∀x~∃yTxy
viii*	∃xyz((Fxy & Fyz) &~(Fxz∨Fyx)) ⊢ ∀x∃yFyx → ∀x~Fxx
ix*	∀x∃yFxy, ∃x~∀yGyx, ∃xyFxy ↔ ∃xy(Gyx & ~Gxy)
	⊢ ∃y(Gxy ∨ Gyx)
x*	∃x∃yFxy ↔ ~∃xGxx, ∀y∃xGyx ⊢ ∀x~Fxx

Exercise 4.3.2 Establish whether each of the following sequents is valid or invalid with either a proof or a countermodel.

i $\forall x(Fx \rightarrow \sim Gx), \exists x(Gx \ \& \sim Fx) \vdash \sim \exists xFx \lor \forall x \sim Gx$

ii $\forall x(Fx \rightarrow \sim Gx), \exists x(Gx \ \& \ Fx) \vdash \sim \exists xFx \lor \forall x \sim Gx$

iii $\exists x(Fx \rightarrow Gx) \rightarrow \exists x(Fx \ \& \sim Hx)$
                               $\vdash \exists x(Fx \ \& \ Gx) \rightarrow \sim \forall x(Gx \rightarrow Hx)$

iv $\exists x(Fx \rightarrow Gx) \rightarrow \exists x(Fx \ \& \sim Hx)$
                               $\vdash \exists x(Fx \ \& \ Gx) \rightarrow \forall x(Gx \rightarrow Hx)$

v $\exists x(Fx \lor P), P \leftrightarrow \sim \exists xGx, \sim \exists x(Fx \ \& \ Gx),$
                $\forall x(Hx \rightarrow \sim Fx \ \& \sim Gx) \vdash P \lor \forall x(Hx \rightarrow P)$

vi $\forall x(Fx \ \& \ Gx \rightarrow Hx), \exists xFx \vdash \exists x(Gx \rightarrow Hx)$

vii $\forall x(Fx \ \& \sim Gx \rightarrow Hx), \exists xFx \vdash \exists x(Hx \rightarrow \sim Gx)$

viii $\vdash \forall xFx \lor \exists x \sim Gx \rightarrow \sim \exists x(Fx \lor Gx)$

ix $\vdash \forall xFx \lor \exists xGx \rightarrow \exists x(Fx \lor Gx)$

x $\exists x(Fx \lor Gx), \exists xFx \rightarrow \forall xHx, \exists xGx \rightarrow \sim \exists xHx$
                               $\vdash \sim(\exists xHx \ \& \ \exists x \sim Hx)$

xi $\exists x(Fx \lor Gx), \exists xFx \rightarrow \forall xHx, \exists xGx \rightarrow \sim \exists xHx$
                               $\vdash \sim(\forall xHx \lor \forall x \sim Hx)$

xii $\vdash \sim \exists x(Bx \ \& \ \forall y(Sxy \leftrightarrow \sim Syy))$

xiii $\vdash \forall xy(Fxy \rightarrow Fyx) \leftrightarrow \forall xy(Fxy \leftrightarrow Fyx)$

xiv $\vdash \forall xy(Fxy \rightarrow Fyx) \leftrightarrow \forall xy(Fxy \leftrightarrow Fyx)$

xv $\forall xyz(Rxy \& Rxz \rightarrow \sim Ryz) \vdash \sim \forall xRxx$

xvi $\forall xyz(Rxy \& Ryz \rightarrow \sim Rxz) \vdash \forall x \sim Rxx$

xvii $\forall xyz(Fxy \& Fyz \rightarrow Fxz), \forall xy(Fxy \rightarrow Fyx)$
                               $\vdash \forall x \exists yFxy \rightarrow \forall xFxx$

xviii $\forall xyz(Fxy \& Fyz \rightarrow Fxz), \forall x \exists y(Fxy \rightarrow Fyx)$
                               $\vdash \forall x \exists yFxy \rightarrow \forall xFxx$

xix $\exists x \forall y \sim Fxy \vdash \exists x \forall yz(Fxz \rightarrow Fzy)$

xx $\exists x \forall yFxy \vdash \exists x \sim \forall yz(Fxz \rightarrow Fzy)$

4.4   Finite Countermodels with Identity

name   *Definition.* A **NAME EXTENSION** consists of a
extension   single object selected from the universe.

Comment. The introduction of identity statements requires greater care about the different roles played by names in the language of predicate logic (which we refer to as the *object language*) and in the language we use to specify interpretations (referred to as the *metalanguage*). Things may have more than one name in the object language but each must have a unique metalinguistic name in the specification of an interpretation. To mark this distinction, in this section we shall use italicized letters as names in the metalanguage. To reduce the potential for confusion when specifying an interpretation for a set of sentences we also recommend the practice of not using italicized versions of letters already appearing in the sentences.

Comment. Italicized (metalinguistic) names are not part of the language we are studying. Rather, they are *our* names for the things denoted by names in the object language. It is important to bear in mind that although a thing may be named by various names in the object language, each thing has only *one* metalinguistic name. This will aid in the specification of interpretations for wffs containing the identity symbol.

finite   *Definition.* A finite interpretation for a set of sentences
interpretation   containing one-place and many-place predicates as
                      well as the identity symbol consists of the following:

- A finite universe, or domain.
- Extensions for all the predicates appearing in the sentences.
- Extensions for the names appearing in the sentences.
- Truth value specifications for the sentence letters appearing in the sentences.

identity truth   Identity statements of the form α=β are true if and on-
valuations   ly if the extension of α is the extension of β.

Comment. Because an object never has more than one metalinguistic name, identity statements occurring in expansions are true if and only if they are of the form α=α.

Example.
The expansion of a sentence containing the identity symbol can only proceed given both the universe and the name extensions. Given the universe

  U: {c, d}

and name extensions

  a: c
  b: c

the expansion of the wff

  ∀x(Fxa → x≠b)

requires first the replacement of the object language names with their metalanguage equivalents, yielding:

$\forall x(Fxc \rightarrow x{\neq}c)$.

Then expansion proceeds by the normal method, to yield:

$(Fcc \rightarrow c{\neq}c)$ & $(Fdc \rightarrow d{\neq}c)$.

Finally, given the predicate extension

F: $\{\langle c, d \rangle, \langle d, c \rangle\}$

the conjunction can be seen to be true given the falsity of the antecedent of the left conditional and the truth of both antecedent and consequent on the right.

Exercise 4.4   Construct countermodels for the following sequents.

i* $a{=}b, c{=}d \vdash a{=}c$

ii $Fa, a{\neq}b \vdash {\sim}Fb$

iii $\forall x \exists y\ x{=}y \vdash \exists y \forall x\ y{=}x$

iv $\exists x(x{\neq}a \rightarrow Fx), a{=}b \vdash Fb$

v* $\exists xy((Fx\ \&\ Fy)\ \&\ x \neq y) \vdash \forall x Fx$

vi $\forall xy(Fx\ \&\ Gy \rightarrow x{=}y) \vdash {\sim}\exists x(Fx\ \&\ Gx)$

vii $\exists x(x{\neq}a \rightarrow Fx \vee Gx) \vdash \exists x(Fx \vee Gx \rightarrow x{\neq}a)$

viii $\forall xy(Fxy \rightarrow y{=}x) \vdash \exists x Fxx$

ix* $\exists x \forall y(Fxy \leftrightarrow x{\neq}y) \vdash \forall xyz((Fxy\ \&\ Fxz) \rightarrow y{=}z)$

x $\forall xy((Fx\ \&\ Fy) \rightarrow x{\neq}y)$

$\vdash \forall xyz(((Fx\ \&\ Fy)\ \&\ Fz)\ \&\ ((x{\neq}y\ \&\ y{\neq}z)\ \&\ x{\neq}z))$

4.5   **Infinite Countermodels**

infinite
countermodel

Comment. Sometimes an invalid argument cannot be shown invalid by means of a *finite* countermodel. Such cases require an **INFINITE COUNTERMODEL**, i.e., one with an *infinite* number of objects in its domain.

Comment. A formal treatment of infinite sets requires an advanced course in set theory. Nonetheless it is possible to exploit knowledge about sets of numbers to construct counterexamples for invalid arguments that require infinite models. The wffs of predicate logic can be given interpretations in terms of arithmetical relationships in infinite domains such as the natural numbers or the set of positive and negative integers.

For ease of exposition we will take the natural numbers (0,1,2,3, etc.) as the infinite domain to be used. (This set is denoted **N**.) Note also that we cannot use expansions to construct countermodels, since an expansion for an infinite number of objects would involve infinitely long sentences.

numerical   *Definition.* A **NUMERICAL COUNTERMODEL** to
countermodel an argument is a countermodel whose universe is **N**.

Example.
$\forall xyz(Rxy \ \& \ Ryz \rightarrow Rxz)$, $\forall xy(Rxy \rightarrow \sim Ryx)$,
$\forall x \sim Rxx$, $\forall x \exists y Rxy \vdash \exists y \forall x Rxy$

Model:
    U: **N**
    R: $\{\langle m,n \rangle$ such that $m < n\}$
    (also written $\{\langle m,n \rangle : m < n\}$)
That is, Rxy means that x is strictly less than y.

The four premises are true, since (i) if x is less than y
and y is less than z then x is less than z, (ii) if x is less
than y then y is not less than x, (iii) no number is less
than itself, and (iv) for any number there is a greater.
The conclusion is false, however, since it says that
there is a number greater than any number. That is, no
number y is such that for every number x, $\langle x,y \rangle$
belongs to R.

It can be shown that only an infinite model can make
all four premises true. A given single object bears R to
something (fourth premise), but it doesn't bear R to
itself (third premise), so a second object must be
present. This second object bears R to something
(fourth premise), but it doesn't bear R to the first
object (second premise) and it doesn't bear R to itself
(third premise). Hence, a third object must be present.
This third object doesn't bear R to itself (third

premise), and it doesn't bear R to the second object (second premise), and since the first object bears R to this third object as well as the second (first premise), the third doesn't bear R to the first (second premise). But this third object bears R to *something* (fourth premise), hence a fourth object must be present, and so forth. Thus, the four premises require an infinite universe.

Exercise 4.5.1 Return to any invalid sequent of this chapter, and give a numerical countermodel for it. (Of course, up to this point infinite models were not *necessary* for demonstrating invalidity, but they are possible.)

Exercise 4.5.2 Give numerical countermodels to the following sequents.

i* $\forall xyz(Fxy \ \& \ Fyz \rightarrow Fxz), \ \forall x \exists y Fxy \vdash \exists x Fxx$

ii* $\forall x \exists y \forall z(Fxy \ \& \ (Fyz \rightarrow Fxz)) \vdash \exists x Fxx$

iii* $\forall x \exists y Fxy, \ \forall xyz(Fxy \ \& \ Fyz \rightarrow Fxz), \ \forall x{\sim}Fxx$
$$\vdash \forall xy(Gx \ \& \ {\sim}Gy \rightarrow Fxy \lor Fyx)$$

iv* $\forall x \exists yz(Fxy \ \& \ Fzx), \ \forall xyz(Fxy \ \& \ Fyz \rightarrow Fxz)$
$$\vdash \exists xy(Fxy \ \& \ Fyx)$$

v* $\forall x{\sim}Fxx, \ \forall x \exists y \forall z(Fxy \ \& \ (Fyz \rightarrow Fxz))$
$$\vdash \forall xyz(Fxy \ \& \ Fyz \rightarrow Fxz)$$

vi* $\forall xyz(Gxy \ \& \ Gyz \rightarrow Gxz), \ \forall xy(Gxy \rightarrow {\sim}Gyx),$
$\forall x \exists y Gyx, \ \forall x(x{\neq}a \rightarrow Gxa) \vdash \exists y \forall x(x{\neq}y \rightarrow Gyx)$

Answers to Selected Exercises

Note: In almost all cases the answers given are not the only correct answers possible.

Chapter 1

Exercise 1.1

i	False
ii	False
iii	False
iv	True
v	False
vi	True
vii	False
viii	True
ix	True
x	False

Exercise 1.2.1

i	Atomic Sentence
ii	Not wff
iii	Not wff
iv	Conditional: Antecedent A; Consequent B
v	Not wff
vi	Conditional: Antecedent A; Consequent (B → C)
vii	Conditional: Antecedent (P & Q); Consequent R
viii	Disjunction: Left disjunct (A & B); Right disjunct (C → (D ↔ G))
ix	Negation
x	Not wff; requires outer parentheses to be a disjunction
xi	Not wff
xii	Not wff
xiii	Conjunction: Left conjunct ~(P & P); Right conjunct (P ↔ (Q ∨ ~Q))
xiv	Biconditional: Left side ~((B ∨ P) & C); Right side ((D ∨ ~G) → H)
xv	Not wff

Exercise 1.2.2

iv	A → B
vi	A → (B → C)
vii	P & Q → R
viii	(A & B) ∨ (C → (D ↔ G))
xiii	~(P & P) ∨ (P ↔ Q ∨ ~Q)
xiv	~((B ∨ P) & C) ↔ D ∨ ~G → H

Exercise 1.2.3

i	Unambiguous: (P ↔ (~Q ∨ R))
ii	Unambiguous: ((P ∨ Q) → (R & S))
iii	Unambiguous: (((P ∨ Q) → R) ↔ S)
iv	Ambiguous
v	Ambiguous
vi	Ambiguous
vii	Unambiguous: ((P & Q) ↔ (~R ∨ S))
viii	Ambiguous
ix	Unambiguous: ((P → (Q & ~R)) ↔ ((~S ∨ T) → U))
x	Ambiguous

Exercise 1.3

1	P & ~Q
2	~P → ~T
3	P → T
4	T → P
5	~P ∨ T(or ~T → ~P)
6	(T → P) → ~U
7	(Q & ~S) → R
8	~(P ∨ R) → ~T
9	~T ∨ (P ∨ R) (or the same as 8)
10	(P & R) → T
11	T & ~(P ∨ R)
12	R → (Q → P)
13	T → U
14	~T → ~(P ∨ R)

15        $(Q \rightarrow R)$ & $(P \rightarrow Q) \rightarrow (P \rightarrow R)$

16        $(P \vee R)$ & $\sim(P$ & $R) \rightarrow Q$

17        $(P$ & $Q)$ & $\sim R \rightarrow (\sim T$ & $(S$ & $U))$

18        $T \leftrightarrow S$

19        $\sim U \rightarrow (\sim P \vee Q)$ or $(\sim U \rightarrow (\sim Q \rightarrow \sim P))$

20        $((P \rightarrow Q) \rightarrow P) \rightarrow P$

21   P & $Q \rightarrow R$

22        $\sim Q$ & S

23        $(\sim Q \rightarrow \sim R) \vee \sim P$ or $(P \rightarrow (\sim Q \rightarrow \sim R))$

24        $(T$ & $\sim P) \rightarrow \sim R$

25        $(T$ & $P) \rightarrow (R$ & $\sim Q)$

Exercise 1.4.1

ii. $P \vee Q, \sim Q \vee R, \sim P \vdash$ [the sentence at line 5]

1	(1)	$P \vee Q$	A
2	(2)	$\sim Q \vee R$	A
3	(3)	$\sim P$	A
1,3	(4)	Q	1,3 $\vee$E
1,2,3	(5)	R	2,4 $\vee$E

or

1,2,3	(5)	$(\sim Q \vee R)$ & Q	2,4 &I

or

1,2,3	(5)	Q & $(\sim Q \vee R)$	2,4 &I

iii. $P \rightarrow Q, P \vee Q \vdash Q$

1	(1)	$P \rightarrow Q$	A
2	(2)	$P \vee Q$	A
3	(3)	$\sim Q$	A
2,3	(4)	P	2,3 $\vee$E
1,2,3	(5)	Q	1,4 $\rightarrow$E
1,2	(6)	Q	3,5 RAA (3)

iv $\sim P \leftrightarrow Q, \sim Q \vee R \vdash \sim P \rightarrow R$

1	(1)	$\sim P \leftrightarrow Q$	A
2	(2)	$\sim P$	A
3	(3)	$\sim Q \vee R$	A
1	(4)	$\sim P \rightarrow Q$	$1 \leftrightarrow E$
1,2	(5)	Q	$2,4 \rightarrow E$
1,2,3	(6)	R	$3,5 \vee E$
1,3	(7)	$\sim P \rightarrow R$	$6 \rightarrow I \ (2)$

Exercise 1.4.2

S1 $P \vee \sim R, \sim R \rightarrow S, \sim P \vdash S$

1	(1)	$P \vee \sim R$	A
2	(2)	$\sim R \rightarrow S$	A
3	(3)	$\sim P$	A
1,3	(4)	$\sim R$	$1,3 \vee E$
1,2,3	(5)	S	$2,4 \rightarrow E$

S3 $P \rightarrow \sim Q, \sim Q \vee R \rightarrow \sim S, P \ \& \ T \vdash \sim S$

1	(1)	$P \rightarrow \sim Q$	A
2	(2)	$\sim Q \vee R \rightarrow \sim S$	A
3	(3)	$P \ \& \ T$	A
3	(4)	P	$3 \ \&E$
1,3	(5)	$\sim Q$	$1,4 \rightarrow E$
1,3	(6)	$\sim Q \vee R$	$5 \vee I$
1,2,3	(7)	$\sim S$	$2,6 \rightarrow E$

S4 $P \ \& \ (Q \ \& \ R), P \ \& \ R \rightarrow \sim S, S \vee T \vdash T$

1	(1)	$P \ \& \ (Q \ \& \ R)$	A
2	(2)	$P \ \& \ R \rightarrow \sim S$	A
3	(3)	$S \vee T$	A
1	(4)	P	$1 \ \&E$
1	(5)	$Q \ \& \ R$	$1 \ \&E$
1	(6)	R	$5 \ \&E$
1	(7)	$P \ \& \ R$	$4,6 \ \&I$
1,2	(8)	$\sim S$	$2,7 \rightarrow E$
1,2,3	(9)	T	$3,8 \vee E$

S7   ~P, R ∨ ~P ↔ P ∨ Q ⊢ Q
1   (1)   ~P   A
2   (2)   R ∨ ~P ↔ P ∨ Q   A
1   (3)   R ∨ ~P   1 ∨I
2   (4)   R ∨ ~P → P ∨ Q   2 ↔E
1,2   (5)   P ∨ Q   3,4 →E
1,2   (6)   Q   1,5 ∨E

S9   ~P → Q & R, ~P ∨ S → ~T, U & ~P ⊢ (U & R) & ~T
1   (1)   ~P → Q & R   A
2   (2)   ~P ∨ S → ~T   A
3   (3)   U & ~P   A
3   (4)   ~P   3 &E
1,3   (5)   Q & R   1,4 →E
1,3   (6)   R   5 &E
3   (7)   U   3 &E
1,3   (8)   U & R   6,7 &I
3   (9)   ~P ∨ S   4 ∨I
2,3   (10)   ~T   2,9 →E
1,2,3   (11)   (U & R) & ~T   8,10 &I

Exercise 1.5.1

S11   P ⊣⊢ ~~P

(a)   P ⊢ ~~P
1   (1)   P   A
2   (2)   ~P   A
1   (3)   ~~P   1,2 RAA (2)

(b)   ~~P ⊢ P
1   (1)   ~~P   A
2   (2)   ~P   A
1   (3)   P   1,2 RAA (2)

S12   P → Q, ~Q ⊢ ~P
1   (1)   P → Q   A
2   (2)   ~Q   A
3   (3)   P   A
1,3   (4)   Q   1,3 →E
1,2   (5)   ~P   2,4 RAA (3)

S14   ~P → Q, ~Q ⊢ P
1   (1)   ~P → Q   A
2   (2)   ~Q   A
3   (3)   ~P   A
1,3   (4)   Q   1,3 →E
1,2   (5)   P   2,4 RAA (3)

S16   P → Q, Q → R ⊢ P → R
1   (1)   P → Q   A
2   (2)   Q → R   A
3   (3)   P   A
1,3   (4)   Q   1,3 →E
1,2,3   (5)   R   2,4 →E
1,2   (6)   P → R   5 →I (3)

S17   P ⊢ Q → P
1   (1)   P   A
2   (2)   Q   A
1   (3)   Q → P   1 →I (2)

S18   ~P ⊢ P → Q
1   (1)   ~P   A
2   (2)   P   A
3   (3)   ~Q   A
1,2   (4)   Q   1,2 RAA (3)
1   (5)   P → Q   4 →I (2)

S21   ~P ∨ Q ⊣⊢ P → Q

(a)   ~P ∨ Q ⊢ P → Q

1	(1)	~P ∨ Q	A
2	(2)	P	A
1,2	(3)	Q	1,2 ∨E
1	(4)	P → Q	3 →I (2)

(b)   P → Q ⊢ ~P ∨ Q

1	(1)	P → Q	A
2	(2)	~(~P ∨ Q)	A
3	(3)	~P	A
3	(4)	~P ∨ Q	3 ∨I
2	(5)	P	2,4 RAA (3)
1,2	(6)	Q	1,5 →E
1,2	(7)	~P ∨ Q	6 ∨I
1	(8)	~P ∨ Q	2,7 RAA (2)

S26   P ∨ Q, P → R, Q → S ⊢ R ∨ S

1	(1)	P ∨ Q	A
2	(2)	P → R	A
3	(3)	Q → S	A
4	(4)	~(R ∨ S)	A [for RAA]
5	(5)	~R	A [for RAA]
6	(6)	P	A [for RAA]
2,6	(7)	R	2,6 →E
2,5	(8)	~P	5,7 RAA (6)
1,2,5	(9)	Q	1,8 ∨E
1,2,3,5	(10)	S	3,9 →E
1,2,3,5	(11)	R ∨ S	10 ∨I
1,2,3,4	(12)	R	4,11 RAA (5)
1,2,3,4	(13)	R ∨ S	12 ∨I
1,2,3	(14)	R ∨ S	4,13 RAA (4)

S28   ~(P ∨ Q) ⊣⊢ ~P & ~Q

(a)   ~(P ∨ Q) ⊢ ~P & ~Q
1   (1)   ~(P ∨ Q)   A
2   (2)   P   A [for RAA]
2   (3)   P ∨ Q   2 ∨I
1   (4)   ~P   1,3 RAA (2)
5   (5)   Q   A [for RAA]
5   (6)   P ∨ Q   5 ∨I
1   (7)   ~Q   1,6 RAA (5)
1   (8)   ~P & ~Q   4,7 &I

(b)   ~P & ~Q ⊢ ~(P ∨ Q)
1   (1)   ~P & ~Q   A
1   (2)   ~P   1 &E
1   (3)   ~Q   1 &E
4   (4)   P ∨ Q   A
1,4   (5)   Q   2,4 ∨E
1   (6)   ~(P ∨ Q)   3,5 RAA (4)

S32   ~(P → Q) ⊣⊢ P & ~Q

(a)   ~(P → Q) ⊢ P & ~Q
1   (1)   ~(P → Q)   A
2   (2)   ~P   A
3   (3)   P   A
4   (4)   ~Q   A
2,3   (5)   Q   2,3 RAA (4)
2   (6)   P → Q   5 →I (3)
1   (7)   P   1,6 RAA (2)
8   (8)   Q   A
8   (9)   P → Q   8 →I (3)
1   (10)   ~Q   1,9 RAA (8)
1   (11)   P & ~Q   7,10 &I

(b)   P & ~Q ⊢ ~(P → Q)
1   (1)   P & ~Q   A
2   (2)   P → Q   A [for RAA]
1   (3)   P   1 &E

1,2	(4)	Q	2,3 →E
1	(5)	~Q	1 &E
1	(6)	~(P → Q)	4,5 RAA (2)

S37   P ∨ Q ⊣⊢ Q ∨ P

(a)   P ∨ Q ⊢ Q ∨ P

1	(1)	P ∨ Q	A
2	(2)	~(Q ∨ P)	A
3	(3)	~P	A
1,3	(4)	Q	1,3 ∨E
1,3	(5)	Q ∨ P	4 ∨I
1,2	(6)	P	2,5 RAA (3)
1,2	(7)	Q ∨ P	6 ∨I
1	(8)	Q ∨ P	2,7 RAA (2)

(b)   Q ∨ P ⊢ P ∨ Q

1	(1)	Q ∨ P	A
2	(2)	~(P ∨ Q)	A
3	(3)	~P	A
1,3	(4)	Q	1,3 ∨E
1,3	(5)	P ∨ Q	4 ∨I
1,2	(6)	P	2,5 RAA (3)
1,2	(7)	P ∨ Q	6 ∨I
1	(8)	P ∨ Q	2,7 RAA (2)

S38   P ↔ Q ⊣⊢ Q ↔ P

(a)   P ↔ Q ⊢ Q ↔ P

1	(1)	P ↔ Q	A
1	(2)	P → Q	1 ↔E
1	(3)	Q → P	1 ↔E
1	(4)	Q ↔ P	2,3 ↔I

(b)   Q ↔ P ⊢ P ↔ Q

| 1 | (1) | Q ↔ P | A |
| 1 | (2) | Q → P | 1 ↔E |

1	(3).	P → Q	1 ↔E
1	(4)	P ↔ Q	2,3 ↔I

S40   P & (Q & R) ⊣⊢ (P & Q) & R

(a)   P & (Q & R) ⊢ (P & Q) & R

1	(1)	P & (Q & R)	A
1	(2)	P	1 &E
1	(3)	Q & R	1 &E
1	(4)	Q	3 &E
1	(5)	R	3 &E
1	(6)	P & Q	2,4 &I
1	(7)	(P & Q) & R	5,6 &I

(b)   (P & Q) & R ⊢ P & (Q & R)

1	(1)	(P & Q) & R	A
1	(2)	P & Q	1 &E
1	(3)	R	1 &E
1	(4)	P	2 &E
1	(5)	Q	2 &E
1	(6)	Q & R	3,5 &I
1	(7)	P & (Q & R)	4,6 &I

S41   P ∨ (Q ∨ R) ⊣⊢ (P ∨ Q) ∨ R

(a)   P ∨ (Q ∨ R) ⊢ (P ∨ Q) ∨ R

1	(1)	P ∨ (Q ∨ R)	A
2	(2)	~((P ∨ Q) ∨ R)	A
3	(3)	~P	A
1,3	(4)	Q ∨ R	1,3 ∨E
5	(5)	~Q	A
1,3,5	(6)	R	4,5 ∨E
1,3,5	(7)	(P ∨ Q) ∨ R	6 ∨I
1,2,5	(8)	P	2,7 RAA (3)
1,2,5	(9)	P ∨ Q	8 ∨I
1,2,5	(10)	(P ∨ Q) ∨ R	9 ∨I
1,2	(11)	Q	2,10 RAA (5)
1,2	(12)	P ∨ Q	11 ∨I
1,2	(13)	(P ∨ Q) ∨ R	12 ∨I
1	(14)	(P ∨ Q) ∨ R	2,13 RAA (2)

(b)		$(P \lor Q) \lor R \vdash P \lor (Q \lor R)$	
1	(1)	$(P \lor Q) \lor R$	A
2	(2)	$\sim(P \lor (Q \lor R))$	A
3	(3)	P	A
3	(4)	$P \lor (Q \lor R)$	3 $\lor$I
2	(5)	$\sim P$	2,4 RAA (3)
6	(6)	R	A
6	(7)	$Q \lor R$	6 $\lor$I
6	(8)	$P \lor (Q \lor R)$	7 $\lor$I
2	(9)	$\sim R$	2,8 RAA (6)
1,2	(10)	$P \lor Q$	1,9 $\lor$E
1,2	(11)	Q	5,10 $\lor$E
1,2	(12)	$Q \lor R$	11 $\lor$I
1,2	(13)	$P \lor (Q \lor R)$	12 $\lor$I
1	(14)	$P \lor (Q \lor R)$	2,13 RAA (2)

S42		$P \& (Q \lor R) \dashv\vdash (P \& Q) \lor (P \& R)$	
(a)		$P \& (Q \lor R) \vdash (P \& Q) \lor (P \& R)$	
1	(1)	$P \& (Q \lor R)$	A
2	(2)	$\sim((P \& Q) \lor (P \& R))$	A [for RAA]
1	(3)	P	1 &E
1	(4)	$Q \lor R$	1 &E
5	(5)	Q	A [for RAA]
1,5	(6)	$P \& Q$	3,5 &I
1,5	(7)	$(P \& Q) \lor (P \& R)$	6 $\lor$I
1,2	(8)	$\sim Q$	2,7 RAA (5)
1,2	(9)	R	4,8 $\lor$E
1,2	(10)	$P \& R$	3,9 &I
1,2	(11)	$(P \& Q) \lor (P \& R)$	10 $\lor$I
1	(12)	$(P \& Q) \lor (P \& R)$	2,11 RAA (2)

(b)		$(P \& Q) \lor (P \& R) \vdash P \& (Q \lor R)$	
1	(1)	$(P \& Q) \lor (P \& R)$	A
2	(2)	$\sim P$	A [for RAA]
3	(3)	$P \& Q$	A [for RAA]
3	(4)	P	3 &E

2	(5)	~(P & Q)	2,4 RAA (3)
1,2	(6)	P & R	1,5 ∨E
1,2	(7)	P	6 &E
1	(8)	P	2,7 RAA (2)
9	(9)	~(Q ∨ R)	A [for RAA]
10	(10)	~Q	A
3	(11)	Q	3 &E
10	(12)	~(P & Q)	10,11 RAA (3)
1,10	(13)	P & R	1,12 ∨E
1,10	(14)	R	13 &E
1,10	(15)	Q ∨ R	14 ∨I
1,9	(16)	Q	9,15 RAA (10)
1,9	(17)	Q ∨ R	16 ∨I
1	(18)	Q ∨ R	9,17 RAA (9)
1	(19)	P & (Q ∨ R)	8,18 &I

Exercise 1.5.2

S53   P ↔ Q ⊣⊢ (P & Q) ∨ (~P & ~Q)

(a)		P ↔ Q ⊢ (P & Q) ∨ (~P & ~Q)	
1	(1)	P ↔ Q	A
1	(2)	P → Q	1 ↔E
1	(3)	Q → P	1 ↔E
4	(4)	~((P & Q) ∨ (~P & ~Q))	A
5	(5)	~P	A
6	(6)	Q	A
1,6	(7)	P	3,6 →E
1,5	(8)	~Q	5,7 RAA (6)
1,5	(9)	~P & ~Q	5,8 &I
1,5	(10)	(P & Q) ∨ (~P & ~Q)	9 ∨I
1,4	(11)	P	4,10 RAA (5)
1,4	(12)	Q	2,11 →E
1,4	(13)	P & Q	11,12 &I
1,4	(14)	(P & Q) ∨ (~P & ~Q)	13 ∨I
1	(15)	(P & Q) ∨ (~P & ~Q)	4,14 RAA (4)

(b)		(P & Q) ∨ (~P & ~Q) ⊢ P ↔ Q	
1	(1)	(P & Q) ∨ (~P & ~Q)	A
2	(2)	P	A

3	(3)	~Q	A
4	(4)	P & Q	A
4	(5)	Q	4 &E
3	(6)	~(P & Q)	3,5 RAA (4)
1,3	(7)	~P & ~Q	1,6 ∨E
1,3	(8)	~P	7 &E
1,2	(9)	Q	2,8 RAA (3)
1	(10)	P → Q	9 →I (2)
11	(11)	Q	A [for →I]
12	(12)	~P & ~Q	A [for RAA]
12	(13)	~Q	12 &E
11	(14)	~(~P & ~Q)	11,13 RAA (12)
1,11	(15)	P & Q	1,14 ∨E
1,11	(16)	P	15 &E
1	(17)	Q → P	16 →I (11)
1	(18)	P ↔ Q	10,17 ↔I

S55		(~P ∨ Q) & R, Q → S ⊢ P → (R → S)	
1	(1)	(~P ∨ Q) & R	A
2	(2)	Q → S	A
3	(3)	P	A
4	(4)	R	A
1	(5)	~P ∨ Q	1 &E
1,3	(6)	Q	3,5 ∨E
1,2,3	(7)	S	2,6 →E
1,2,3	(8)	R → S	7 →I (4)
1,2	(9)	P → (R → S)	8 →I (3)

S56		Q & R, Q → P ∨ S, ~(S & R) ⊢ P	
1	(1)	Q & R	A
2	(2)	Q → P ∨ S	A
3	(3)	~(S & R)	A
1	(4)	Q	1 &E
1	(5)	R	1 &E
1,2	(6)	P ∨ S	2,4 →E
7	(7)	~P	A [for RAA]
1,2,7	(8)	S	6,7 ∨E
1,2,7	(9)	S & R	5,8 &I
1,2,3	(10)	P	3,9 RAA (7)

Exercise 1.5.3

	Form	*Substitution*
i	Trans	(P/R; Q/S)
ii	HS	(P/~P; Q/Q ∨ R; R/S)
ii	∨ Comm	(P/P & Q; Q/R)
iv	Dist &/∨	(P/P ∨ Q; Q/~R; R/~S)
v	DN	(P/R ∨ S)
vi	Neg→	(P/P ∨ R; Q/S)
vii	∨→	(P/P; Q/Q ∨ R)
viii	TC	(P/~(P & Q); Q/R)
ix	DM	(P/P & Q; Q/R & S)
x	Sim Dil	(P/P; Q/R ∨ S; R/Q & R)

Exercise 1.5.4

S66		P ↔ Q ⊢ P ∨ Q → P & Q	
1	(1)	P ↔ Q	A
2	(2)	P ∨ Q	A [for →I]
3	(3)	P	A
1,3	(4)	Q	1,3 BP
1,3	(5)	P & Q	3,4 &I
1	(6)	P → P & Q	5 →I (3)
7	(7)	Q	A
1,7	(8)	P	1,7 BP
1,7	(9)	P & Q	7,8 &I
1	(10)	Q → P & Q	9 →I (7)
1,2	(11)	P & Q	2,6,10 Sim Dil
1	(12)	P ∨ Q → P & Q	11 →I (2)

S67		P ↔ Q ⊣⊢ ~(P ∨ Q) ∨ ~(~P ∨ ~Q)	
(a)		P ↔ Q ⊢ ~(P ∨ Q) ∨ ~(~P ∨ ~Q)	
1	(1)	P ↔ Q	A
1	(2)	P → Q	1 ↔E
1	(3)	Q → P	1 ↔E
4	(4)	P ∨ Q	A
4	(5)	~P → Q	4 ∨→
1,4	(6)	Q	2,5 Spec Dil

4	(7)	~Q → P	4 ∨→
1,4	(8)	P	3,7 Spec Dil
1,4	(9)	P & Q	6,8 &I
1,4	(10)	~(~P ∨ ~Q)	9 DM
1	(11)	P ∨ Q → ~(~P ∨ ~Q)	10 →I (4)
1	(12)	~(P ∨ Q) ∨ ~(~P ∨ ~Q)	11 ∨→

(b)   ~(P ∨ Q) ∨ ~(~P ∨ ~Q) ⊢ P ↔ Q

1	(1)	~(P ∨ Q) ∨ ~(~P ∨ ~Q)	A
2	(2)	P	A [for →I]
2	(3)	P ∨ Q	2 ∨I
1,2	(4)	~(~P ∨ ~Q)	1,3 ∨E
1,2	(5)	P & Q	4 DM
1,2	(6)	Q	5 &E
1	(7)	P → Q	6 →I (2)
8	(8)	Q	A [for →I]
8	(9)	P ∨ Q	8 ∨I
1,8	(10)	~(~P ∨ ~Q)	1,9 ∨E
1,8	(11)	P & Q	10 DM
1,8	(12)	P	11 &E
1	(13)	Q → P	12 →I (8)
1	(14)	P ↔ Q	7,13 ↔I

S73   (P & Q) ∨ (R ∨ S) ⊢ ((P & Q) ∨ R) ∨ S

1	(1)	(P & Q) ∨ (R ∨ S)	A
2	(2)	P & Q	A
2	(3)	(P & Q) ∨ R	2 ∨I
2	(4)	((P & Q) ∨ R) ∨ S	3 ∨I
	(5)	P & Q → ((P & Q) ∨ R) ∨ S	4 →I (2)
6	(6)	R ∨ S	A
7	(7)	R	A
7	(8)	(P & Q) ∨ R	7 ∨I
	(9)	R → (P & Q) ∨ R	8 →I (7)
	(10)	S → S	Id
6	(11)	((P & Q) ∨ R) ∨ S	6,9,10 Com Dil
	(12)	R ∨ S → ((P & Q) ∨ R) ∨ S	11 →I (6)
1	(13)	((P & Q) ∨ R) ∨ S	1,5,12 Sim Dil

S76   P ∨ Q, (Q → R) & (~P ∨ S), Q & R → T ⊢ T ∨ S

1	(1)	P ∨ Q	A
2	(2)	(Q → R) & (~P ∨ S)	A
3	(3)	Q & R → T	A
2	(4)	Q → R	2 &E
2	(5)	~P ∨ S	2 &E
6	(6)	~T	A [for →I]
3,6	(7)	~(Q & R)	3,6 MTT
3,6	(8)	Q → ~R	7 Neg→
2,3,6	(9)	~Q	4,8 IA
1,2,3,6	(10)	P	1,9 ∨E
1,2,3,6	(11)	S	5,10 ∨E
1,2,3	(12)	~T → S	11 →I (6)
1,2,3	(13)	T ∨ S	12 ∨→

S78   P ∨ Q, P → (R → ~S), (~R ↔ T) → ~P ⊢ S & T → Q

1	(1)	P ∨ Q	A
2	(2)	P → (R → ~S)	A
3	(3)	(~R ↔ T) → ~P	A
4	(4)	S & T	A [for →I]
5	(5)	P	A [for RAA]
2,5	(6)	R → ~S	2,5 →E
3,5	(7)	~(~R ↔ T)	3,5 MTT
4	(8)	S	4 &E
2,4,5	(9)	~R	6,8 MTT
4	(10)	T	4 &E
4	(11)	~R → T	10 TC
2,4,5	(12)	T → ~R	9 TC
2,4,5	(13)	~R ↔ T	11,12 ↔I
2,3,4	(14)	~P	7,13 RAA (5)
1,2,3,4	(15)	Q	1,14 ∨E
1,2,3	(16)	S & T → Q	15 →I (4)

S79 $(P \leftrightarrow \sim Q) \rightarrow \sim R, (\sim P \& S) \lor (Q \& T), S \lor T \rightarrow R \vdash Q \rightarrow P$

1	(1)	$(P \leftrightarrow \sim Q) \rightarrow \sim R$	A
2	(2)	$(\sim P \& S) \lor (Q \& T)$	A
3	(3)	$S \lor T \rightarrow R$	A
4	(4)	Q	A [for $\rightarrow$I]
5	(5)	$\sim P$	A [for RAA]
5	(6)	$P \rightarrow \sim Q$	5 FA
4	(7)	$\sim Q \rightarrow P$	4 FA
4,5	(8)	$P \leftrightarrow \sim Q$	6,7 $\leftrightarrow$I
1,4,5	(9)	$\sim R$	1,8 $\rightarrow$E
1,3,4,5	(10)	$\sim(S \lor T)$	3,9 MTT
1,3,4,5	(11)	$\sim S \& \sim T$	10 DM
1,3,4,5	(12)	$\sim S$	11 &E
1,3,4,5	(13)	$P \lor \sim S$	12 $\lor$I
1,3,4,5	(14)	$\sim(\sim P \& \sim\sim S)$	13 DM
15	(15)	$\sim P \& S$	A
15	(16)	$\sim P$	15 &E
15	(17)	S	15 &E
15	(18)	$\sim\sim S$	17 DN
15	(19)	$\sim P \& \sim\sim S$	16,18 &I
	(20)	$\sim P \& S \rightarrow \sim P \& \sim\sim S$	19 $\rightarrow$I (15)
1,3,4,5	(21)	$\sim(\sim P \& S)$	14,20 MTT
1,2,3,4,5	(22)	$Q \& T$	2,21 $\lor$E
1,2,3,4,5	(23)	T	22 &E
1,3,4,5	(24)	$\sim T$	11 &E
1,2,3,4	(25)	P	23,24 RAA (5)
1,2,3	(26)	$Q \rightarrow P$	25 $\rightarrow$I (4)

S80 $\sim S \lor (S \& R), (S \rightarrow R) \rightarrow P \vdash P$

1	(1)	$\sim S \lor (S \& R)$	A
2	(2)	$(S \rightarrow R) \rightarrow P$	A
3	(3)	$\sim S$	A [for $\rightarrow$I]
3	(4)	$S \rightarrow R$	3 FA
	(5)	$\sim S \rightarrow (S \rightarrow R)$	4 $\rightarrow$I (3)
6	(6)	$S \& R$	A
6	(7)	R	6 &E
6	(8)	$S \rightarrow R$	7 TC
	(9)	$S \& R \rightarrow (S \rightarrow R)$	8 $\rightarrow$I (6)

1	(10)	$S \rightarrow R$	1,5,9 Sim Dil
1,2	(11)	P	2,10 $\rightarrow$E

S81		$P \lor (R \lor Q), (R \rightarrow S) \& (Q \rightarrow T), S \lor T \rightarrow P \lor Q, \sim P \vdash Q$	
1	(1)	$P \lor (R \lor Q)$	A
2	(2)	$(R \rightarrow S) \& (Q \rightarrow T)$	A
3	(3)	$S \lor T \rightarrow P \lor Q$	A
4	(4)	$\sim P$	A
1,4	(5)	$R \lor Q$	1,4 $\lor$E
2	(6)	$R \rightarrow S$	2 &E
2	(7)	$Q \rightarrow T$	2 &E
1,2,4	(8)	$S \lor T$	5,6,7 Com Dil
1,2,3,4	(9)	$P \lor Q$	3,8 $\rightarrow$E
1,2,3,4	(10)	Q	4,9 $\lor$E

S82		$(P \rightarrow Q) \rightarrow R, S \rightarrow (\sim Q \rightarrow T) \vdash R \lor \sim T \rightarrow (S \rightarrow R)$	
1	(1)	$(P \rightarrow Q) \rightarrow R$	A
2	(2)	$S \rightarrow (\sim Q \rightarrow T)$	A
3	(3)	$R \lor \sim T$	A [for $\rightarrow$I]
4	(4)	R	A
4	(5)	$S \rightarrow R$	4 TC
	(6)	$R \rightarrow (S \rightarrow R)$	5 $\rightarrow$I (4)
7	(7)	$\sim T$	A
2	(8)	$S \& \sim Q \rightarrow T$	2 Exp/imp
2,7	(9)	$\sim(S \& \sim Q)$	7,8 MTT
2,7	(10)	$\sim S \lor \sim\sim Q$	9 DM
11	(11)	$\sim S$	A
11	(12)	$S \rightarrow R$	11 FA
	(13)	$\sim S \rightarrow (S \rightarrow R)$	12 $\rightarrow$I (11)
14	(14)	$\sim\sim Q$	A
14	(15)	Q	14 DN
14	(16)	$P \rightarrow Q$	15 TC
1,14	(17)	R	1,16 $\rightarrow$E
1,14	(18)	$S \rightarrow R$	17 TC
1	(19)	$\sim\sim Q \rightarrow (S \rightarrow R)$	18 $\rightarrow$I (14)
1,2,7	(20)	$S \rightarrow R$	10,13,19 SimDil
1,2	(21)	$\sim T \rightarrow (S \rightarrow R)$	20 $\rightarrow$I (7)

| 1,2,3 | (22) | $S \rightarrow R$ | 3,6,21 Sim Dil |
| 1,2 | (23) | $R \vee {\sim}T \rightarrow (S \rightarrow R)$ | 22 $\rightarrow$I (3) |

S83		$P \& Q \rightarrow R \vee S \vdash (P \rightarrow R) \vee (Q \rightarrow S)$	
1	(1)	$P \& Q \rightarrow R \vee S$	A
2	(2)	${\sim}(P \rightarrow R)$	A [for $\rightarrow$I]
2	(3)	$P \& {\sim}R$	2 Neg$\rightarrow$
4	(4)	Q	A [for $\rightarrow$I]
2	(5)	P	3 &E
2,4	(6)	$P \& Q$	4,5 &I
1,2,4	(7)	$R \vee S$	1,6 $\rightarrow$E
2	(8)	${\sim}R$	3 &E
1,2,4	(9)	S	7,8 $\vee$E
1,2	(10)	$Q \rightarrow S$	9 $\rightarrow$I (4)
1	(11)	${\sim}(P \rightarrow R) \rightarrow (Q \rightarrow S)$	10 $\rightarrow$I (2)
1	(12)	$(P \rightarrow R) \vee (Q \rightarrow S)$	11 $\vee\rightarrow$

S84		$(P \rightarrow Q) \& (R \rightarrow P), (P \vee R) \& {\sim}(Q \& R) \vdash (P \& Q) \& {\sim}R$	
1	(1)	$(P \rightarrow Q) \& (R \rightarrow P)$	A
2	(2)	$(P \vee R) \& {\sim}(Q \& R)$	A
1	(3)	$P \rightarrow Q$	1 &E
1	(4)	$R \rightarrow P$	1 &E
2	(5)	$P \vee R$	2 &E
2	(6)	${\sim}(Q \& R)$	2 &E
2	(7)	${\sim}Q \vee {\sim}R$	6 DM
2	(8)	${\sim}P \rightarrow R$	5 $\vee\rightarrow$
1	(9)	${\sim}P \rightarrow {\sim}R$	4 Trans
1,2	(10)	${\sim}{\sim}P$	8.9 IA
1,2	(11)	P	10 DN
1	(12)	$R \rightarrow Q$	3,4 HS
1	(13)	${\sim}Q \rightarrow {\sim}R$	12 Trans
2	(14)	$Q \rightarrow {\sim}R$	7 $\vee\rightarrow$
1,2	(15)	${\sim}R$	13,14 Spec Dil
1,2	(16)	Q	3,11 $\rightarrow$E
1,2	(17)	$P \& Q$	11,16 &I
1,2	(18)	$(P \& Q) \& {\sim}R$	15,17 &I

S85   P & Q → (R ∨ S) & ~(R & S), R & Q → S,

                    S → ((R & Q) ∨ (~R & ~Q)) ∨ ~P ⊢ P → ~Q

1	(1)	P & Q → (R ∨ S) & ~(R & S)	A
2	(2)	R & Q → S	A
3	(3)	S → ((R & Q) ∨ (~R & ~Q)) ∨ ~P	A
4	(4)	P	A [for →I]
5	(5)	Q	A [for RAA]
4,5	(6)	P & Q	4,5 &I
1,4,5	(7)	(R ∨ S) & ~(R & S)	1,6 →E
1,4,5	(8)	R ∨ S	7 &E
1,4,5	(9)	~(R & S)	7 &E
1,4,5	(10)	R → ~S	9 Neg→
11	(11)	R	A
5,11	(12)	R & Q	5,11 &I
2,5,11	(13)	S	2,12 →E
2,5	(14)	R → S	13 →I (11)
1,2,4,5	(15)	~R	10,14 IA
1,2,4,5	(16)	S	8,15 ∨E
1,2,3,4,5	(17)	((R & Q) ∨ (~R & ~Q)) ∨ ~P	3,16 →E
1,2,3,4,5	(18)	(R & Q) ∨ (~R & ~Q)	4,17 ∨E
5	(19)	~R → Q	5 TC
5	(20)	~(~R & ~Q)	19 Neg→
1,2,3,4,5	(21)	R & Q	18,20 ∨E
1,2,3,4,5	(22)	R	21 &E
1,2,3,4	(23)	~Q	15,22 RAA (5)
1,2,3	(24)	P → ~Q	22 →I (4)

Exercise 1.6.1

T1   ⊢ P → P
| 1 | (1) | P | A |
| | (2) | P → P | 1 →I (1) |

T2   ⊢ P ∨ ~P
(i) primitive rules only
1	(1)	~(P ∨ ~P)	A [for RAA]
2	(2)	P	A [for RAA]
2	(3)	P ∨ ~P	2 ∨I

1	(4)	~P	1,3 RAA (2)
1	(5)	P ∨ ~P	4 ∨I
	(6)	P ∨ ~P	1,5 RAA (1)

(ii) derived rules allowed

1	(1)	~P	A
	(2)	~P → ~P	1 →I (1)
	(3)	P ∨ ~P	2 ∨→

T4   ⊢ P → (Q → P)
(i) primitive rules only

1	(1)	P	A [for →I]
2	(2)	Q	A [for →I]
1	(3)	Q → P	1 →I (2)
	(4)	P → (Q → P)	3 →I (1)

(ii) derived rules allowed

1	(1)	P	A
1	(2)	Q → P	1 TC
	(3)	P → (Q → P)	2 →I (1)

T5   ⊢ (P → Q) ∨ (Q → P)
(i) primitive rules only

1	(1)	~((P → Q) ∨ (Q → P))	A [for RAA]
2	(2)	P → Q	A [for RAA]
2	(3)	(P → Q) ∨ (Q → P)	2 ∨I
1	(4)	~(P → Q)	1,3 RAA (2)
5	(5)	~P	A [for RAA]
6	(6)	P	A [for →I]
7	(7)	~Q	A [for RAA]
5,6	(8)	Q	5,6 RAA (7)
5	(9)	P → Q	8 →I (6)
1	(10)	P	4,9 RAA (5)
11	(11)	Q	A [for →I]
1	(12)	Q → P	10 →I (11)
1	(13)	(P → Q) ∨ (Q → P)	12 ∨I
	(14)	(P → Q) ∨ (Q → P)	1,13 RAA (1)

(ii) derived rules allowed

1	(1)	~((P → Q) ∨ (Q → P))	A
1	(2)	~(P → Q) & ~(Q → P)	1 DM
1	(3)	~(P → Q)	2 &E
1	(4)	~(Q → P)	2 &E
1	(5)	P & ~Q	3 Neg →
1	(6)	Q & ~P	4 Neg →
1	(7)	P	5 &E
1	(8)	~P	6 &E
	(9)	(P → Q) ∨ (Q → P)	7,8 RAA (1)

T8   ⊢ ~(P ↔ Q) ↔ (~P ↔ Q)

(i) primitive rules only

1	(1)	~(P ↔ Q)	A [for →I]
2	(2)	~P	A [for →I]
3	(3)	~Q	A
2	(4)	~Q → ~P	2 →I (3)
5	(5)	P	A [for →I]
2,3	(6)	~P	3,4 →E
2,5	(7)	Q	5,6 RAA (3)
2	(8)	P → Q	7 →I (5)
3	(9)	~P → ~Q	3 →I (2)
10	(10)	Q	A [for →I]
11	(11)	~P	A [for RAA]
3,11	(12)	~Q	9,11 →E
3,10	(13)	P	10,12 RAA (11)
3	(14)	Q → P	13 →I (10)
2,3	(15)	P ↔ Q	8,14 ↔I
1,2	(16)	Q	1,15 RAA (3)
1	(17)	~P → Q	16 →I (2)
10	(18)	P → Q	10 →I (5)
5	(19)	Q → P	5 →I (10)
5,10	(20)	P ↔ Q	18,19 ↔I
1,10	(21)	~P	1,20 RAA (5)
1	(22)	Q → ~P	21 →I (10)
1	(23)	~P ↔ Q	17,22 ↔I
	(24)	~(P ↔ Q) → (~P ↔ Q)	23 →I (1)
25	(25)	~P ↔ Q	A [for →I]

25	(26)	~P → Q	25 ↔E
25	(27)	Q → ~P	25 ↔E
28	(28)	P ↔ Q	A [for RAA]
28	(29)	P → Q	28 ↔E
28	(30)	Q → P	28 ↔E
10,28	(31)	P	10,30 →E
10,25	(32)	~P	10,27 →E
25,28	(33)	~Q	31,32 RAA (10)
5,28	(34)	Q	5,29 →E
25,28	(35)	~P	33,34 RAA (5)
25,28	(36)	Q	26,35 →E
25	(37)	~(P ↔ Q)	33,36 RAA (28)
	(38)	(~P ↔ Q) → ~(P ↔ Q)	37 →I (25)
	(39)	~(P ↔ Q) ↔ (~P ↔ Q)	24,38 ↔I

T9   ⊢ ((P → Q) → P) → P
(i) primitive rules only

1	(1)	(P → Q) → P	A [for →I]
2	(2)	~P	A [for RAA]
3	(3)	P → Q	A
1,3	(4)	P	1,3 →E
1,2	(5)	~(P → Q)	2,4 RAA (3)
6	(6)	P	A [for →I]
7	(7)	~Q	A [for RAA]
2,6	(8)	Q	2,6 RAA (7)
2	(9)	P → Q	8 →I (6)
1	(10)	P	5,9 RAA (2)
	(11)	((P → Q) → P) → P	10 →I (1)

(ii) derived rules allowed

1	(1)	~(((P → Q) → P) → P)	A
1	(2)	((P → Q) → P) & ~P	1 Neg →
1	(3)	(P → Q) → P	2 &E
1	(4)	~P	2 &E
1	(5)	~(P → Q)	3,4 MTT
1	(6)	P & ~Q	5 Neg →
1	(7)	P	6 &E
	(8)	((P → Q) → P) → P	4,7 RAA (1)

T10   ⊢ (P → Q) ∨ (Q → R)

(i) primitive rules only

1	(1)	~((P → Q) ∨ (Q → R))	A [for RAA]
2	(2)	(P → Q)	A
2	(3)	(P → Q) ∨ (Q → R)	2 ∨I
1	(4)	~(P → Q)	1,3 RAA (2)
5	(5)	Q	A [for →I]
6	(6)	~R	A [for RAA]
7	(7)	P	A
5	(8)	P → Q	5 →I (7)
1,5	(9)	R	4,8 RAA (6)
1	(10)	Q → R	9 →I (5)
1	(11)	(P → Q) ∨ (Q → R)	10 ∨I
	(12)	(P → Q) ∨ (Q → R)	1,11 RAA (1)

(ii) derived rules allowed

1	(1)	~(P → Q)	A
1	(2)	P & ~Q	1 Neg →
1	(3)	~Q	2 &E
1	(4)	Q → R	3 FA
	(5)	~(P → Q) → (Q → R)	4 →I (1)
	(6)	(P → Q) ∨ (Q → R)	5 ∨→

(ii) alternative proof using derived rules

1	(1)	Q	A
1	(2)	P → Q	1 TC
1	(3)	(P → Q) ∨ (Q → R)	2 ∨I
	(4)	Q → (P → Q) ∨ (Q → R)	3 →I (1)
5	(5)	~Q	A
5	(6)	Q → R	5 FA
5	(7)	(P → Q) ∨ (Q → R)	6 ∨I
	(8)	~Q → (P → Q) ∨ (Q → R)	7 →I (5)
	(9)	(P → Q) ∨ (Q → R)	4,8 Spec Dil

T11   ⊢ (P ↔ Q) ↔ (~P ↔ ~Q)

(i) primitive rules only

1	(1)	P ↔ Q	A [for →I]
1	(2)	P → Q	1 ↔E
1	(3)	Q → P	1 ↔E
4	(4)	~P	A [for →I]
5	(5)	Q	A [for RAA]
1,5	(6)	P	3,5 →E
1,4	(7)	~Q	4,6 RAA (5)
1	(8)	~P → ~Q	7 →I (4)
9	(9)	~Q	A [for →I]
10	(10)	P	A [for RAA]
1,10	(11)	Q	2,10 →E
1,9	(12)	~P	9,11 RAA (10)
1	(13)	~Q → ~P	12 →I (9)
1	(14)	~P ↔ ~Q	8,13 ↔I
	(15)	(P ↔ Q) → (~P ↔ ~Q)	14 →I (1)
16	(16)	~P ↔ ~Q	A [for →I]
16	(17)	~P → ~Q	16 ↔E
16	(18)	~Q → ~P	16 ↔E
19	(19)	P	A [for →I]
20	(20)	~Q	A [for RAA]
16,20	(21)	~P	18,20 →E
16,19	(22)	Q	19,21 RAA (20)
16	(23)	P → Q	22 →I (19)
24	(24)	Q	A [for →I]
25	(25)	~P	A [for RAA]
16,25	(26)	~Q	17,25 →E
16,24	(27)	P	24,26 RAA (25)
16	(28)	Q → P	27 →I (24)
16	(29)	P ↔ Q	23,28 ↔I
	(30)	(~P ↔ ~Q) → (P ↔ Q)	29 →I (16)
	(31)	(P ↔ Q) ↔ (~P ↔ ~Q)	15,30 ↔I

(ii) derived rules allowed

1	(1)	P ↔ Q	A
1	(2)	Q ↔ P	1 Comm
1	(3)	~P ↔ ~Q	2 Bitrans

	(4)	$(P \leftrightarrow Q) \to (\sim P \leftrightarrow \sim Q)$	$3 \to I (2)$
5	(5)	$\sim P \leftrightarrow \sim Q$	A
5	(6)	$Q \leftrightarrow P$	5 Bitrans
5	(7)	$P \leftrightarrow Q$	6 Comm
	(8)	$(\sim P \leftrightarrow \sim Q) \to (P \leftrightarrow Q)$	$7 \to I (5)$
	(9)	$(P \leftrightarrow Q) \leftrightarrow (\sim P \leftrightarrow \sim Q)$	$4,8 \leftrightarrow I$

T12 $\vdash (\sim P \to Q) \& (R \to Q) \leftrightarrow (P \to R) \to Q$

(i) primitive rules only

1	(1)	$(\sim P \to Q) \& (R \to Q)$	A
1	(2)	$\sim P \to Q$	1 &E
1	(3)	$R \to Q$	1 &E
4	(4)	$P \to R$	A [for $\to$I]
5	(5)	$\sim Q$	A [for RAA]
6	(6)	$\sim P$	A
1,6	(7)	Q	$2,6 \to E$
1,5	(8)	P	5,7 RAA (6)
1,4,5	(9)	R	$4,8 \to E$
1,4,5	(10)	Q	$3,9 \to E$
1,4	(11)	Q	5,10 RAA (5)
1	(12)	$(P \to R) \to Q$	$11 \to I (4)$
	(13)	$(\sim P \to Q) \& (R \to Q) \to ((P \to R) \to Q)$	$12 \to I (1)$
14	(14)	$(P \to R) \to Q$	A
15	(15)	$\sim P$	A
16	(16)	P	A
17	(17)	$\sim R$	A
15,16	(18)	R	15,16 RAA (17)
15	(19)	$P \to R$	$18 \to I (16)$
14,15	(20)	Q	$14,19 \to E$
14	(21)	$\sim P \to Q$	$20 \to I (15)$
22	(22)	R	A
22	(23)	$P \to R$	$22 \to I (16)$
14,22	(24)	Q	$14,23 \to E$
14	(25)	$R \to Q$	$24 \to I (22)$
14	(26)	$(\sim P \to Q) \& (R \to Q)$	21,25 &I
	(27)	$((P \to R) \to Q) \to (\sim P \to Q) \& (R \to Q)$	$26 \to I (14)$
	(28)	$(\sim P \to Q) \& (R \to Q) \leftrightarrow (P \to R) \to Q$	$13,27 \leftrightarrow I$

(ii) derived rules allowed

1	(1)	(~P → Q) & (R → Q)	A
1	(2)	~P → Q	1 &E
1	(3)	R → Q	1 &E
4	(4)	P → R	A
1,4	(5)	P → Q	3,4 HS
1,4	(6)	Q	2,5 Spec Dil
1	(7)	(P → R) → Q	6 →I (4)
	(8)	(~P → R) & (R → Q) → ((P → R) → Q)	7 →I (1)
9	(9)	(P → R) → Q	A
10	(10)	~P	A
10	(11)	P → R	10 FA
9,10	(12)	Q	9,11 →E
9	(13)	~P → Q	12 →I (10)
14	(14)	R	A
14	(15)	P → R	14 TC
9,14	(16)	Q	9,15 →E
9	(17)	R → Q	16 →E (14)
9	(18)	(~P → Q) & (R → Q)	13,17 &I
	(19)	((P → R) → Q) → (~P → Q) & (R → Q)	18 →I (9)
	(20)	(~P → Q) & (R → Q) ↔ (P → R) → Q	8,19 ↔I

T13	⊢ P ↔ P & P		
1	(1)	P	A
1	(2)	P & P	1,1 &I
	(3)	P → P & P	2 →I (1)
4	(4)	P & P	A
4	(5)	P	4 &E
	(6)	P & P → P	5 →I (4)
	(7)	P ↔ P & P	3,6 ↔I

T14	⊢ P ↔ P ∨ P		
1	(1)	P	A
1	(2)	P ∨ P	1 ∨I
	(3)	P → P ∨ P	2 →I (1)
4	(4)	P ∨ P	A
5	(5)	~P	A [for RAA]
4,5	(6)	P	4,5 ∨E

4	(7)	P	5,6 RAA (5)
	(8)	$P \vee P \to P$	$7 \to I$ (4)
	(9)	$P \leftrightarrow P \vee P$	$3,8 \leftrightarrow I$

T17 $\vdash (P \leftrightarrow Q) \& (R \leftrightarrow S) \to (P \vee R \leftrightarrow Q \vee S)$
(i) primitive rules only

1	(1)	$(P \leftrightarrow Q) \& (R \leftrightarrow S)$	A
1	(2)	$P \leftrightarrow Q$	1 &E
1	(3)	$P \to Q$	$2 \leftrightarrow E$
1	(4)	$Q \to P$	$2 \leftrightarrow E$
1	(5)	$R \leftrightarrow S$	1 &E
1	(6)	$R \to S$	$5 \leftrightarrow E$
1	(7)	$S \to R$	$5 \leftrightarrow E$
8	(8)	$P \vee R$	A [for $\to I$]
9	(9)	$\sim(Q \vee S)$	A [for RAA]
10	(10)	Q	A
10	(11)	$Q \vee S$	10 $\vee$I
9	(12)	$\sim Q$	9,11 RAA (10)
13	(13)	P	A
1,13	(14)	Q	$3,13 \to E$
1,9	(15)	$\sim P$	12,14 RAA (13)
1,8,9	(16)	R	8,15 $\vee$E
1,8,9	(17)	S	$6,16 \to E$
1,8,9	(18)	$Q \vee S$	17 $\vee$I
1,8	(19)	$Q \vee S$	9,18 RAA (9)
1	(20)	$P \vee R \to Q \vee S$	$19 \to I$ (8)
21	(21)	$Q \vee S$	A
22	(22)	$\sim(P \vee R)$	A
23	(23)	P	A
23	(24)	$P \vee R$	23 $\vee$I
22	(25)	$\sim P$	22,24 RAA (23)
26	(26)	Q	A
1,26	(27)	P	$4,26 \to E$
1,22	(28)	$\sim Q$	25,27 RAA (26)
1,21,22	(29)	S	21,28 $\vee$E
1,21,22	(30)	R	$7,29 \to E$
1,21,22	(31)	$P \vee R$	30 $\vee$I
1,21	(32)	$P \vee R$	22,31 RAA (22)

1	(33)	$Q \lor S \to P \lor R$	$32 \to I$ (21)
1	(34)	$P \lor R \leftrightarrow Q \lor S$	$20,33 \leftrightarrow I$
	(35)	$(P \leftrightarrow Q) \mathbin{\&} (R \leftrightarrow S) \to (P \lor R \leftrightarrow Q \lor S)$	$34 \to I$ (1)

(ii) derived rules allowed

1	(1)	$(P \leftrightarrow Q) \mathbin{\&} (R \leftrightarrow S)$	A
1	(2)	$P \leftrightarrow Q$	1 &E
1	(3)	$R \leftrightarrow S$	1 &E
4	(4)	$P \lor R$	A
1	(5)	$P \to Q$	$2 \leftrightarrow E$
1	(6)	$R \to S$	$3 \leftrightarrow E$
1,4	(7)	$Q \lor S$	4,5,6 Com Dil
1	(8)	$P \lor R \to Q \lor S$	$7 \to I$ (4)
9	(9)	$Q \lor S$	A
1	(10)	$Q \to P$	$2 \leftrightarrow E$
1	(11)	$S \to R$	$3 \leftrightarrow E$
1,9	(12)	$P \lor R$	9,10,11 Com Dil
1	(13)	$Q \lor S \to P \lor R$	$12 \to I$ (9)
1	(14)	$P \lor R \leftrightarrow Q \lor S$	$8,13 \leftrightarrow I$
	(15)	$(P \leftrightarrow Q) \mathbin{\&} (R \leftrightarrow S) \to (P \lor R \leftrightarrow Q \lor S)$	$14 \to I$ (1)

T19 $\vdash (P \leftrightarrow Q) \to ((R \to P) \leftrightarrow (R \to Q)) \mathbin{\&} ((P \to R) \leftrightarrow (Q \to R))$
(i) primitive rules only

1	(1)	$P \leftrightarrow Q$	A [for $\to$I]
1	(2)	$P \to Q$	$1 \leftrightarrow E$
1	(3)	$Q \to P$	$1 \leftrightarrow E$
4	(4)	$R \to P$	A [for $\to$I]
5	(5)	R	A [for $\to$I]
4,5	(6)	P	$4,5 \to E$
1,4,5	(7)	Q	$2,6 \to E$
1,4	(8)	$R \to Q$	$7 \to I$ (5)
1	(9)	$(R \to P) \to (R \to Q)$	$8 \to I$ (4)
10	(10)	$R \to Q$	A
11	(11)	R	A
10,11	(12)	Q	$10,11 \to E$
1,10,11	(13)	P	$3,12 \to E$
1,10	(14)	$R \to P$	$13 \to I$ (11)

1	(15)	$(R \rightarrow Q) \rightarrow (R \rightarrow P)$	$14 \rightarrow I$ (10)
1	(16)	$(R \rightarrow P) \leftrightarrow (R \rightarrow Q)$	$9,15 \leftrightarrow I$
17	(17)	$P \rightarrow R$	A
18	(18)	Q	A
1,18	(19)	P	$3,18 \rightarrow E$
1,17,18	(20)	R	$17,19 \rightarrow E$
1,17	(21)	$Q \rightarrow R$	$20 \rightarrow I$ (18)
1	(22)	$(P \rightarrow R) \rightarrow (Q \rightarrow R)$	$21 \rightarrow I$ (17)
23	(23)	$Q \rightarrow R$	A
24	(24)	P	A
1,24	(25)	Q	$2,24 \rightarrow E$
1,23,24	(26)	R	$23,25 \rightarrow E$
1,23	(27)	$P \rightarrow R$	$26 \rightarrow I$ (24)
1	(28)	$(Q \rightarrow R) \rightarrow (P \rightarrow R)$	$27 \rightarrow I$ (23)
1	(29)	$(P \rightarrow R) \leftrightarrow (Q \rightarrow R)$	$22,28 \leftrightarrow I$
1	(30)	$((R \rightarrow P) \leftrightarrow (R \rightarrow Q)) \& ((P \rightarrow R) \leftrightarrow (Q \rightarrow R))$	$16,29 \& I$
	(31)	$(P \leftrightarrow Q) \rightarrow$	$30 \rightarrow I$ (1)
		$((R \rightarrow P) \leftrightarrow (R \rightarrow Q)) \& ((P \rightarrow R) \leftrightarrow (Q \rightarrow R))$	

(ii) derived rules allowed

1	(1)	$P \leftrightarrow Q$	A
1	(2)	$P \rightarrow Q$	$1 \leftrightarrow E$
1	(3)	$Q \rightarrow P$	$1 \leftrightarrow E$
4	(4)	$R \rightarrow P$	A
1,4	(5)	$R \rightarrow Q$	2,4 HS
1	(6)	$(R \rightarrow P) \rightarrow (R \rightarrow Q)$	$5 \rightarrow I$ (4)
7	(7)	$R \rightarrow Q$	A
1,7	(8)	$R \rightarrow P$	3,7 HS
1	(9)	$(R \rightarrow Q) \rightarrow (R \rightarrow P)$	$8 \rightarrow I$ (7)
1	(10)	$(R \rightarrow P) \leftrightarrow (R \rightarrow Q)$	$6,9 \leftrightarrow I$
11	(11)	$P \rightarrow R$	A
1,11	(12)	$Q \rightarrow R$	3,11 HS
1	(13)	$(P \rightarrow R) \rightarrow (Q \rightarrow R)$	$12 \rightarrow I$ (11)
14	(14)	$Q \rightarrow R$	A
1,14	(15)	$P \rightarrow R$	2,14 HS
1	(16)	$(Q \rightarrow R) \rightarrow (P \rightarrow R)$	$15 \rightarrow I$ (14)
1	(17)	$(P \rightarrow R) \leftrightarrow (Q \rightarrow R)$	$13,16 \leftrightarrow I$

1	(18)	$((R \rightarrow P) \leftrightarrow (R \rightarrow Q)) \& ((P \rightarrow R) \leftrightarrow (Q \rightarrow R))$	10,17 &I
	(19)	$(P \leftrightarrow Q) \rightarrow$	18 $\rightarrow$I (1)
		$((R \rightarrow P) \leftrightarrow (R \rightarrow Q)) \& ((P \rightarrow R) \leftrightarrow (Q \rightarrow R))$	

T21 $\vdash (P \leftrightarrow Q) \rightarrow (R \vee P \leftrightarrow R \vee Q)$

(i) primitive rules only

1	(1)	$P \leftrightarrow Q$	A
1	(2)	$P \rightarrow Q$	1 $\leftrightarrow$E
1	(3)	$Q \rightarrow P$	1 $\leftrightarrow$E
4	(4)	$R \vee P$	A
5	(5)	$\sim(R \vee Q)$	A
6	(6)	R	A
6	(7)	$R \vee Q$	6 $\vee$I
5	(8)	$\sim$R	5,7 RAA (6)
4,5	(9)	P	4,8 $\vee$E
1,4,5	(10)	Q	2,9 $\rightarrow$E
1,4,5	(11)	$R \vee Q$	10 $\vee$I
1,4	(12)	$R \vee Q$	5,11 RAA (5)
1	(13)	$R \vee P \rightarrow R \vee Q$	12 $\rightarrow$I (4)
14	(14)	$R \vee Q$	A
15	(15)	$\sim(R \vee P)$	A
16	(16)	R	A
16	(17)	$R \vee P$	16 $\vee$I
15	(18)	$\sim$R	15,17 RAA (16)
14,15	(19)	Q	14,18 $\vee$E
1,14,15	(20)	P	3,19 $\rightarrow$E
1,14,15	(21)	$R \vee P$	20 $\vee$I
1,14	(22)	$R \vee P$	15,21 RAA (15)
1	(23)	$R \vee Q \rightarrow R \vee P$	22 $\rightarrow$I (14)
1	(24)	$R \vee P \leftrightarrow R \vee Q$	13,23 $\leftrightarrow$I
	(25)	$(P \leftrightarrow Q) \rightarrow (R \vee P \leftrightarrow R \vee Q)$	24 $\rightarrow$I (1)

(ii) derived rules allowed

1	(1)	$P \leftrightarrow Q$	A
1	(2)	$P \rightarrow Q$	1 $\leftrightarrow$E
1	(3)	$Q \rightarrow P$	1 $\leftrightarrow$E
4	(4)	$R \vee P$	A

4	(5)	$\sim R \rightarrow P$	$4 \lor \rightarrow$
1,4	(6)	$\sim R \rightarrow Q$	2,5 HS
1,4	(7)	$R \lor Q$	$6 \lor \rightarrow$
1	(8)	$R \lor P \rightarrow R \lor Q$	$7 \rightarrow I (4)$
9	(9)	$R \lor Q$	A
9	(10)	$\sim R \rightarrow Q$	$9 \lor \rightarrow$
1,9	(11)	$\sim R \rightarrow P$	3,10 HS
1,9	(12)	$R \lor P$	$11 \lor \rightarrow$
1	(13)	$R \lor Q \rightarrow R \lor P$	$12 \rightarrow I (9)$
1	(14)	$R \lor P \leftrightarrow R \lor Q$	$8,13 \leftrightarrow I$
	(15)	$(P \leftrightarrow Q) \rightarrow (R \lor P \leftrightarrow R \lor Q)$	$14 \rightarrow I (1)$

T27 $\vdash (P \rightarrow Q) \rightarrow Q \leftrightarrow (Q \rightarrow P) \rightarrow P$

(i) primitive rules only

1	(1)	$(P \rightarrow Q) \rightarrow Q$	A [for $\rightarrow$I]
2	(2)	$Q \rightarrow P$	A [for $\rightarrow$I]
3	(3)	$\sim P$	A [for RAA]
4	(4)	Q	A
2,4	(5)	P	$2,4 \rightarrow$E
2,3	(6)	$\sim Q$	3,5 RAA (4)
7	(7)	$P \rightarrow Q$	A
1,7	(8)	Q	$1,7 \rightarrow$E
1,2,3	(9)	$\sim(P \rightarrow Q)$	6,8 RAA (7)
10	(10)	P	A
10	(11)	$P \lor Q$	$10 \lor$I
3,10	(12)	Q	$3,11 \lor$E
3	(13)	$P \rightarrow Q$	$12 \rightarrow I (10)$
1,2	(14)	P	9,13 RAA (3)
1	(15)	$(Q \rightarrow P) \rightarrow P$	$14 \rightarrow I (2)$
	(16)	$((P \rightarrow Q) \rightarrow Q) \rightarrow ((Q \rightarrow P) \rightarrow P)$	$15 \rightarrow I (1)$
17	(17)	$(Q \rightarrow P) \rightarrow P$	A [for $\rightarrow$I]
18	(18)	$P \rightarrow Q$	A [for $\rightarrow$I]
19	(19)	$\sim Q$	A [for RAA]
20	(20)	P	A
18,20	(21)	Q	$18,20 \rightarrow$E
18,19	(22)	$\sim P$	19,21 RAA (20)
23	(23)	$Q \rightarrow P$	A
17,23	(24)	P	$17,23 \rightarrow$E

17,18,19	(25)	~(Q → P)	22,24 RAA (23)
26	(26)	Q	A
26	(27)	Q ∨ P	26 ∨I
19,26	(28)	P	19,27 ∨E
19	(29)	Q → P	28 →I (26)
17,18	(30)	Q	25,29 RAA (19)
17	(31)	(P → Q) → Q	30 →I (18)
	(32)	((Q → P) → P) → ((P → Q) → Q)	31 →I (17)
	(33)	(P → Q) → Q ↔ (Q → P) → P	16,32 ↔I

(ii) derived rules allowed

1	(1)	~(((P → Q) → Q) → ((Q → P) → P))	A
1	(2)	((P → Q) → Q) & ~((Q → P) → P)	1 Neg →
1	(3)	(P → Q) → Q	2 &E
1	(4)	~((Q → P) → P)	2 &E
1	(5)	(Q → P) & ~P	4 Neg →
1	(6)	Q → P	5 &E
1	(7)	~P	5 &E
1	(8)	P → Q	7 FA
1	(9)	Q	3,8 →E
1	(10)	P	6,9 →E
	(11)	((P → Q) → Q) → ((Q → P) → P)	7,10 RAA (1)
12	(12)	~(((Q → P) → P) → ((P → Q) → Q)))	A
12	(13)	((Q → P) → P) & ~((P → Q) → Q)	12 Neg →
12	(14)	(Q → P) → P	13 &E
12	(15)	~((P → Q) → Q)	13 &E
12	(16)	(P → Q) & ~Q	15 Neg →
12	(17)	P → Q	16 &E
12	(18)	~Q	16 &E
12	(19)	Q → P	18 FA
12	(20)	P	14,19 →E
12	(21)	Q	17,20 →E
	(22)	((Q → P) → P) → ((P → Q) → Q)	18,21 RAA (12)
	(23)	(P → Q) → Q ↔ (Q → P) → P	11,22 ↔I

T30   ⊢ (P & Q) ∨ (R & S) ↔ ((P ∨ R) & (P ∨ S)) & ((Q ∨ R) & (Q ∨ S))
(i) primitive rules only

1	(1)	(P & Q) ∨ (R & S)	A [for →I]
2	(2)	~(P ∨ R)	A [for RAA]
3	(3)	~(P ∨ S)	A [for RAA]
4	(4)	~P	A
5	(5)	P & Q	A
5	(6)	P	5 &E
4	(7)	~(P & Q)	4,6 RAA (5)
1,4	(8)	R & S	1,7 ∨E
1,4	(9)	R	8 &E
1,4	(10)	S	8 &E
1,4	(11)	P ∨ R	9 ∨I
1,2	(12)	P	2,11 RAA (4)
1,2	(13)	P ∨ R	12 ∨I
1	(14)	P ∨ R	2,13 RAA (2)
1,4	(15)	P ∨ S	10 ∨I
1,3	(16)	P	3,15 RAA (4)
1,3	(17)	P ∨ S	16 ∨I
1	(18)	P ∨ S	3,17 RAA (3)
1	(19)	(P ∨ R) & (P ∨ S)	14,18 &I
20	(20)	~(Q ∨ R)	A [for RAA]
21	(21)	~(Q ∨ S)	A [for RAA]
22	(22)	~Q	A
5	(23)	Q	5 &E
22	(24)	~(P & Q)	22,23 RAA (5)
1,22	(25)	R & S	1,24 ∨E
1,22	(26)	R	25 &E
1,22	(27)	S	25 &E
1,22	(28)	Q ∨ R	26 ∨I
1,20	(29)	Q	20,28 RAA (22)
1,20	(30)	Q ∨ R	28 ∨I
1	(31)	Q ∨ R	20,30 RAA (20)
1,22	(32)	Q ∨ S	27 ∨I
1,21	(33)	Q	21,32 RAA (22)
1,21	(34)	Q ∨ S	33 ∨I
1	(35)	Q ∨ S	21,34 RAA (21)
1	(36)	(Q ∨ R) & (Q ∨ S)	30,35 &I

1	(37)	$((P \lor R) \& (P \lor S)) \& ((Q \lor R) \& (Q \lor S))$	19,36 &I
	(38)	$(P \& Q) \lor (R \& S) \to$	37 →I (1)
		$((P \lor R) \& (P \lor S)) \& ((Q \lor R) \& (Q \lor S))$	
39	(39)	$((P \lor R) \& (P \lor S)) \& ((Q \lor R) \& (Q \lor S))$	A [for →I]
39	(40)	$(P \lor R) \& (P \lor S)$	39 &E
39	(41)	$(Q \lor R) \& (Q \lor S)$	39 &E
39	(42)	$P \lor R$	40 &E
39	(43)	$P \lor S$	40 &E
39	(44)	$Q \lor R$	41 &E
39	(45)	$Q \lor S$	41 &E
46	(46)	$\sim((P \& Q) \lor (R \& S))$	A [for RAA]
47	(47)	P	A
48	(48)	Q	A
47,48	(49)	$P \& Q$	47,48 &I
47,48	(50)	$(P \& Q) \lor (R \& S)$	49 ∨I
46,47	(51)	$\sim Q$	46,50 RAA (48)
39,46,47	(52)	R	44,51 ∨E
39,46,47	(53)	S	45,51 ∨E
39,46,47	(54)	$R \& S$	52,53 &I
39,46,47	(55)	$(P \& Q) \lor (R \& S)$	54 ∨I
39,46	(56)	$\sim P$	46,55 RAA (47)
39,46	(57)	R	42,56 ∨E
39,46	(58)	S	43,56 ∨E
39,46	(59)	$R \& S$	57,58 &I
39,46	(60)	$(P \& Q) \lor (R \& S)$	59 ∨I
39	(61)	$(P \& Q) \lor (R \& S)$	46,60 RAA (46)
	(62)	$((P \lor R) \& (P \lor S)) \& ((Q \lor R) \& (Q \lor S)) \to$	61 →I (39)
		$(P \& Q) \lor (R \& S)$	
	(63)	$(P \& Q) \lor (R \& S) \leftrightarrow$	38,62 ↔I
		$((P \lor R) \& (P \lor S)) \& ((Q \lor R) \& (Q \lor S))$	

(ii) derived rules allowed

1	(1)	$(P \& Q) \lor (R \& S)$	A
1	(2)	$((P \& Q) \lor R) \& ((P \& Q) \lor S)$	1 Dist
1	(3)	$(P \& Q) \lor R$	2 &E
1	(4)	$(P \& Q) \lor S$	2 &E
1	(5)	$(P \lor R) \& (Q \lor R)$	3 Dist
1	(6)	$(P \lor S) \& (Q \lor S)$	4 Dist

1	(7)	P ∨ R	5 &E
1	(8)	P ∨ S	6 &E
1	(9)	(P ∨ R) & (P ∨ S)	7,8 &I
1	(10)	Q ∨ R	5 &E
1	(11)	Q ∨ S	6 &E
1	(12)	(Q ∨ R) & (Q ∨ S)	10,11 &I
1	(13)	((P ∨ R) & (P ∨ S)) & ((Q ∨ R) & (Q ∨ S))	9,12 &I
	(14)	(P & Q) ∨ (R & S) → ((P ∨ R) & (P ∨ S)) & ((Q ∨ R) & (Q ∨ S))	13 →I (1)
15	(15)	((P ∨ R) & (P ∨ S)) & ((Q ∨ R) & (Q ∨ S))	A
15	(16)	(P ∨ R) & (P ∨ S)	15 &E
15	(17)	(Q ∨ R) & (Q ∨ S)	15 &E
15	(18)	P ∨ R	16 &E
15	(19)	P ∨ S	16 &E
15	(20)	Q ∨ R	17 &E
15	(21)	Q ∨ S	17 &E
15	(22)	(P ∨ R) & (Q ∨ R)	18,20 &I
15	(23)	(P ∨ S) & (Q ∨ S)	19,21 &I
15	(24)	(P & Q) ∨ R	22 Dist
15	(25)	(P & Q) ∨ S	23 Dist
15	(26)	((P & Q) ∨ R) & ((P & Q) ∨ S)	24,25 &I
15	(27)	(P & Q) ∨ (R & S)	26 Dist
	(28)	((P ∨ R) & (P ∨ S)) & ((Q ∨ R) & (Q ∨ S)) → (P & Q) ∨ (R & S)	27 →I (15)
	(29)	(P & Q) ∨ (R & S) ↔ ((P ∨ R) & (P ∨ S)) & ((Q ∨ R) & (Q ∨ S))	14,28 ↔I

T31   ⊢ (P ∨ Q) & (R ∨ S) ↔ ((P & R) ∨ (P & S)) ∨ ((Q & R) ∨ (Q & S))

(i) primitive rules only

1	(1)	(P ∨ Q) & (R ∨ S)	A [for →I]
2	(2)	~(((P & R) ∨ (P & S)) ∨ ((Q & R) ∨ (Q & S)))	A [for RAA]
3	(3)	P & R	A
3	(4)	(P & R) ∨ (P & S)	3 ∨I
3	(5)	((P & R) ∨ (P & S)) ∨ ((Q & R) ∨ (Q & S))	4 ∨I
2	(6)	~(P & R)	2,5 RAA (3)
7	(7)	P & S	A

7	(8)	(P & R) ∨ (P & S)	7 ∨I
7	(9)	((P & R) ∨ (P & S)) ∨ ((Q & R) ∨ (Q & S))	8 ∨I
2	(10)	~(P & S)	2,9 RAA (7)
11	(11)	Q & R	A
11	(12)	(Q & R) ∨ (Q & S)	11 ∨I
11	(13)	((P & R) ∨ (P & S)) ∨ ((Q & R) ∨ (Q & S))	12 ∨I
2	(14)	~(Q & R)	2,13 RAA (11)
15	(15)	Q & S	A
15	(16)	(Q & R) ∨ (Q & S)	15 ∨I
15	(17)	((P & R) ∨ (P & S)) ∨ ((Q & R) ∨ (Q & S))	16 ∨I
2	(18)	~(Q & S)	2,17 RAA (15)
1	(19)	P ∨ Q	1 &E
1	(20)	R ∨ S	1 &E
21	(21)	P	A
22	(22)	R	A
21,22	(23)	P & R	21,22 &I
2,21	(24)	~R	6,23 RAA (22)
1,2,21	(25)	S	20,24 ∨E
1,2,21	(26)	P & S	21,25 &I
1,2	(27)	~P	10,26 RAA (21)
1,2	(28)	Q	19,27 ∨E
1,2,22	(29)	Q & R	22,28 &I
1,2	(30)	~R	14,29 RAA (22)
1,2	(31)	S	20,30 ∨E
1,2	(32)	Q & S	28,31 &I
1	(33)	((P & R) ∨ (P & S)) ∨ ((Q & R) ∨ (Q & S))	18,32 RAA (2)
	(34)	(P ∨ Q) & (R ∨ S) → ((P & R) ∨ (P & S)) ∨ ((Q & R) ∨ (Q & S))	33 →I (1)
35	(35)	((P & R) ∨ (P & S)) ∨ ((Q & R) ∨ (Q & S))	A for →I
36	(36)	~(P ∨ Q)	A [for RAA]
37	(37)	(P & R) ∨ (P & S)	A
38	(38)	P & R	A
38	(39)	P	38 &E
38	(40)	P ∨ Q	39 ∨I
36	(41)	~(P & R)	36,40 RAA (38)
36,37	(42)	P & S	37,41 ∨E
36,37	(43)	P	42 &E
36,37	(44)	P ∨ Q	43 ∨I
36	(45)	~((P & R) ∨ (P & S))	36,44 RAA (37)

35,36	(46)	$((Q \& R) \lor (Q \& S))$	35,45 $\lor$E
47	(47)	$Q \& R$	A
47	(48)	Q	47 &E
47	(49)	$P \lor Q$	48 $\lor$I
36	(50)	$\sim(Q \& R)$	36,49 RAA (47)
35,36	(51)	$Q \& S$	46,50 $\lor$E
35,36	(52)	Q	51 &E
35,36	(53)	$P \lor Q$	52 $\lor$I
35	(54)	$P \lor Q$	36,53 RAA (36)
55	(55)	$\sim(R \lor S)$	A [for RAA]
56	(56)	$(Q \& R) \lor (Q \& S)$	A
57	(57)	$Q \& R$	A
57	(58)	R	57 &E
57	(59)	$R \lor S$	58 $\lor$I
55	(60)	$\sim(Q \& R)$	55,58 RAA (57)
55,56	(61)	$Q \& S$	56,60 $\lor$E
55,56	(62)	S	61 &E
55,56	(63)	$R \lor S$	62 $\lor$I
55	(64)	$\sim((Q \& R) \lor (Q \& S))$	55,63 RAA (56)
35,55	(65)	$(P \& R) \lor (P \& S)$	35,64 $\lor$E
66	(66)	$P \& R$	A
66	(67)	R	66 &E
66	(68)	$R \lor S$	67 $\lor$I
55	(69)	$\sim(P \& R)$	55,68 RAA (66)
35,55	(70)	$P \& S$	65,69 $\lor$E
35,55	(71)	S	70 &E
35,55	(72)	$R \lor S$	71 $\lor$I
35	(73)	$R \lor S$	55,72 RAA (55)
35	(74)	$(P \lor Q) \& (R \lor S)$	54,73 &I
	(75)	$((P \& R) \lor (P \& S)) \lor ((Q \& R) \lor (Q \& S)) \rightarrow$ $(P \lor Q) \& (R \lor S)$	74 $\rightarrow$I (35)
	(76)	$(P \lor Q) \& (R \lor S) \leftrightarrow$ $((P \& R) \lor (P \& S)) \lor ((Q \& R) \lor (Q \& S))$	34,75 $\leftrightarrow$I

(ii) derived rules allowed

1	(1)	$(P \lor Q) \& (R \lor S)$	A
1	(2)	$(P \& (R \lor S)) \lor (Q \& (R \lor S))$	1 Dist
3	(3)	$P \& (R \lor S)$	A

3	(4)	(P & R) ∨ (P & S)	3 Dist
	(5)	P & (R ∨ S) → (P & R) ∨ (P & S)	4 →I (3)
6	(6)	Q & (R ∨ S)	A
6	(7)	(Q & R) ∨ (Q & S)	6 Dist
	(8)	Q & (R ∨ S) → (Q & R) ∨ (Q & S)	7 →I (6)
1	(9)	((P & R) ∨ (P & S)) ∨ ((Q & R) ∨ (Q & S))	2,5,8 Com Dil
	(10)	(P ∨ Q) & (R ∨ S) →	9 →I (1)
		((P & R) ∨ (P & S)) ∨ ((Q & R) ∨ (Q & S))	
11	(11)	((P & R) ∨ (P & S)) ∨ ((Q & R) ∨ (Q & S))	A
12	(12)	(P & R) ∨ (P & S)	A
12	(13)	P & (R ∨ S)	12 Dist
12	(14)	P	13 &E
12	(15)	R ∨ S	13 &E
12	(16)	P ∨ Q	14 ∨I
12	(17)	(P ∨ Q) & (R ∨ S)	15,16 &I
	(18)	(P & R) ∨ (P & S) → (P ∨ Q) & (R ∨ S)	17 →I (12)
19	(19)	(Q & R) ∨ (Q & S)	A
19	(20)	Q & (R ∨ S)	19 Dist
19	(21)	Q	20 &E
19	(22)	R ∨ S	20 &E
19	(23)	P ∨ Q	21 ∨I
19	(24)	(P ∨ Q) & (R ∨ S)	22,23 &I
	(25)	(Q & R) ∨ (Q & S) → (P ∨ Q) & (R ∨ S)	24 →I (19)
11	(26)	(P ∨ Q) & (R ∨ S)	11,18,25 Sim Dil
	(27)	((P & R) ∨ (P & S)) ∨ ((Q & R) ∨ (Q & S)) →	26 →I (11)
		(P ∨ Q) & (R ∨ S)	
	(28)	(P ∨ Q) & (R ∨ S) ↔	10,27 ↔I
		((P & R) ∨ (P & S)) ∨ ((Q & R) ∨ (Q & S))	

T32   ⊢ (P → Q) & (R → S) ↔ ((~P & ~R) ∨ (~P & S)) ∨ ((Q & ~R) ∨ (Q & S))

(i) primitive rules only

1	(1)	(P → Q) & (R → S)	A [for →I]
2	(2)	~(((~P & ~R) ∨ (~P & S)) ∨ ((Q & ~R) ∨ (Q & S)))	A [for RAA]
1	(3)	P → Q	1 &E
1	(4)	R → S	1 &E
5	(5)	(~P & ~R) ∨ (~P & S)	A

5	(6)	$((\sim P \,\&\, \sim R) \vee (\sim P \,\&\, S)) \vee ((Q \,\&\, \sim R) \vee (Q \,\&\, S))$	5 $\vee$I
2	(7)	$\sim((\sim P \,\&\, \sim R) \vee (\sim P \,\&\, S))$	2,6 RAA (5)
8	(8)	$(Q \,\&\, \sim R) \vee (Q \,\&\, S)$	A
8	(9)	$((\sim P \,\&\, \sim R) \vee (\sim P \,\&\, S)) \vee ((Q \,\&\, \sim R) \vee (Q \,\&\, S))$	8 $\vee$I
2	(10)	$\sim((Q \,\&\, \sim R) \vee (Q \,\&\, S))$	2,9 RAA (8)
11	(11)	$(\sim P \,\&\, \sim R)$	A
11	(12)	$(\sim P \,\&\, \sim R) \vee (\sim P \,\&\, S)$	11 $\vee$I
2	(13)	$\sim(\sim P \,\&\, \sim R)$	7,12 RAA (11)
14	(14)	$\sim P \,\&\, S$	A
14	(15)	$(\sim P \,\&\, \sim R) \vee (\sim P \,\&\, S)$	14 $\vee$I
2	(16)	$\sim(\sim P \,\&\, S)$	7,15 RAA (14)
17	(17)	$Q \,\&\, \sim R$	A
17	(18)	$(Q \,\&\, \sim R) \vee (Q \,\&\, S)$	17 $\vee$I
2	(19)	$\sim(Q \,\&\, \sim R)$	10,18 RAA (17)
20	(20)	$Q \,\&\, S$	A
20	(21)	$(Q \,\&\, \sim R) \vee (Q \,\&\, S)$	20 $\vee$I
2	(22)	$\sim(Q \,\&\, S)$	10,21 RAA (20)
23	(23)	$\sim P$	A
24	(24)	$\sim R$	A
23,24	(25)	$\sim P \,\&\, \sim R$	23,24 &I
2,23	(26)	R	13,25 RAA (24)
1,2,23	(27)	S	4,26 $\rightarrow$E
1,2,23	(28)	$\sim P \,\&\, S$	23,27 &I
1,2	(29)	P	16,28 RAA (23)
1,2	(30)	Q	3,29 $\rightarrow$E
1,2,24	(31)	$Q \,\&\, \sim R$	24,30 &I
1,2	(32)	R	19,31 RAA (24)
1,2	(33)	S	4,32 $\rightarrow$E
1,2	(34)	$Q \,\&\, S$	30,33 &I
1	(35)	$((\sim P \,\&\, \sim R) \vee (\sim P \,\&\, S)) \vee ((Q \,\&\, \sim R) \vee (Q \,\&\, S))$	22,34 RAA (2)
	(36)	$(P \rightarrow Q) \,\&\, (R \rightarrow S) \rightarrow$	35 $\rightarrow$I (1)
		$((\sim P \,\&\, \sim R) \vee (\sim P \,\&\, S)) \vee ((Q \,\&\, \sim R) \vee (Q \,\&\, S))$	
37	(37)	$((\sim P \,\&\, \sim R) \vee (\sim P \,\&\, S)) \vee ((Q \,\&\, \sim R) \vee (Q \,\&\, S))$	A [for $\rightarrow$I]
38	(38)	P	A [for $\rightarrow$I]
39	(39)	$\sim Q$	A [for RAA]
40	(40)	$Q \,\&\, \sim R$	A
40	(41)	Q	40 &E
39	(42)	$\sim(Q \,\&\, \sim R)$	39,41 RAA (40)
43	(43)	$Q \,\&\, S$	A

43	(44)	Q	43 &E
39	(45)	~(Q & S)	39,44 RAA (43)
46	(46)	(Q & ~R) ∨ (Q & S)	A
39,46	(47)	Q & S	42,46 ∨E
39	(48)	~((Q & ~R) ∨ (Q & S))	45,47 RAA (46)
37,39	(49)	(~P & ~R) ∨ (~P & S)	37,48 ∨E
50	(50)	~P & ~R	A
50	(51)	~P	50 &E
38	(52)	~(~P & ~R)	38,51 RAA (50)
37,38,39	(53)	~P & S	49,52 ∨E
37,38,39	(54)	~P	53 &E
37,38	(55)	Q	38,54 RAA (39)
37	(56)	P → Q	55 →I (38)
57	(57)	R	A [for →I]
58	(58)	~S	A [for RAA]
59	(59)	Q & S	A
59	(60)	S	59 &E
58	(61)	~(Q & S)	58,60 RAA (59)
62	(62)	(Q & ~R) ∨ (Q & S)	A
58,62	(63)	Q & ~R	61,62 ∨E
58,62	(64)	~R	63 &E
57,58	(65)	~((Q & ~R) ∨ (Q & S))	57,64 RAA (62)
37,57,58	(66)	(~P & ~R) ∨ (~P & S)	37,65 ∨E
67	(67)	~P & ~R	A
67	(68)	~R	67 &E
57	(69)	~(~P & ~R)	57,68 RAA (67)
37,57,58	(70)	~P & S	66,69 ∨E
37,57,58	(71)	S	70 &E
37,57	(72)	S	58,71 RAA (58)
37	(73)	R → S	72 →I (57)
37	(74)	(P → Q) & (R → S)	56,73 &I
	(75)	((~P & ~R) ∨ (~P & S)) ∨ ((Q & ~R) ∨ (Q & S)) → 74 →I (37)	
		(P → Q) & (R → S)	
	(76)	(P → Q) & (R → S) ↔	36,75 ↔I
		((~P & ~R) ∨ (~P & S)) ∨ ((Q & ~R) ∨ (Q & S))	

(ii) derived rules allowed

1	(1)	(P → Q) & (R → S)	A
1	(2)	P → Q	1 &E

1	(3)	$R \rightarrow S$	1 &E
1	(4)	$\sim P \vee Q$	2 $\vee\rightarrow$
1	(5)	$\sim R \vee S$	3 $\vee\rightarrow$
1	(6)	$(\sim P \vee Q) \,\&\, (\sim R \vee S)$	4,5 &I
1	(7)	$(\sim P \,\&\, (\sim R \vee S)) \vee (Q \,\&\, (\sim R \vee S))$	6 Dist
8	(8)	$\sim P \,\&\, (\sim R \vee S)$	A
8	(9)	$(\sim P \,\&\, \sim R) \vee (\sim P \,\&\, S)$	8 Dist
	(10)	$\sim P \,\&\, (\sim R \vee S) \rightarrow (\sim P \,\&\, \sim R) \vee (\sim P \,\&\, S)$	9 $\rightarrow$I (8)
11	(11)	$Q \,\&\, (\sim R \vee S)$	A
11	(12)	$(Q \,\&\, \sim R) \vee (Q \,\&\, S)$	11 Dist
	(13)	$Q \,\&\, (\sim R \vee S) \rightarrow (Q \,\&\, \sim R) \vee (Q \,\&\, S)$	12 $\rightarrow$I (11)
1	(14)	$((\sim P \,\&\, \sim R) \vee (\sim P \,\&\, S)) \vee ((Q \,\&\, \sim R) \vee (Q \,\&\, S))$	7,10,13 Sim Dil
	(15)	$(P \rightarrow Q) \,\&\, (R \rightarrow S) \rightarrow$ $((\sim P \,\&\, \sim R) \vee (\sim P \,\&\, S)) \vee ((Q \,\&\, \sim R) \vee (Q \,\&\, S))$	14 $\rightarrow$I (1)
16	(16)	$((\sim P \,\&\, \sim R) \vee (\sim P \,\&\, S)) \vee ((Q \,\&\, \sim R) \vee (Q \,\&\, S))$	A
17	(17)	$(\sim P \,\&\, \sim R) \vee (\sim P \,\&\, S)$	A
17	(18)	$\sim P \,\&\, (\sim R \vee S)$	17 Dist
	(19)	$(\sim P \,\&\, \sim R) \vee (\sim P \,\&\, S) \rightarrow \sim P \,\&\, (\sim R \vee S)$	18 $\rightarrow$I (17)
20	(20)	$(Q \,\&\, \sim R) \vee (Q \,\&\, S)$	A
20	(21)	$Q \,\&\, (\sim R \vee S)$	20 Dist
	(22)	$(Q \,\&\, \sim R) \vee (Q \,\&\, S) \rightarrow Q \,\&\, (\sim R \vee S)$	21 $\rightarrow$I (20)
16	(23)	$(\sim P \,\&\, (\sim R \vee S)) \vee (Q \,\&\, (\sim R \vee S))$	16,19,22 ComDil
16	(24)	$(\sim P \vee Q) \,\&\, (\sim R \vee S)$	23 Dist
16	(25)	$\sim P \vee Q$	24 &E
16	(26)	$\sim R \vee S$	24 &E
16	(27)	$P \rightarrow Q$	25 $\vee\rightarrow$
16	(28)	$R \rightarrow S$	26 $\vee\rightarrow$
16	(29)	$(P \rightarrow Q) \,\&\, (R \rightarrow S)$	27,28 &E
	(30)	$((\sim P \,\&\, \sim R) \vee (\sim P \,\&\, S)) \vee ((Q \,\&\, \sim R) \vee (Q \,\&\, S)) \rightarrow$ $(P \rightarrow Q) \,\&\, (R \rightarrow S)$	29 $\rightarrow$I (16)
	(31)	$(P \rightarrow Q) \,\&\, (R \rightarrow S) \leftrightarrow$ $((\sim P \,\&\, \sim R) \vee (\sim P \,\&\, S)) \vee ((Q \,\&\, \sim R) \vee (Q \,\&\, S))$	15,30 $\leftrightarrow$I

Chapter 2

Exercise 2.1

i

P Q	P ∨ (~P ∨ Q)
T T	T F T
T F	T F F
F T	T T T
F F	T T T

ii

P Q	~(P & Q) ∨ P
T T	F T T
T F	T F T
F T	T F T
F F	T F T

iii

P Q	~(P → Q) → P
T T	F T T
T F	T F T
F T	F T T
F F	F T T

iv

P Q	(P ∨ Q) ∨ (~P & Q)
T T	T T F F
T F	T T F F
F T	T T T T
F F	F F T F

v

P Q R	P ∨ Q → R ∨ ~P
T T T	T T T F
T T F	T F F F
T F T	T T T F
T F F	T F F F
F T T	T T T T
F T F	T T T T
F F T	F T T T
F F F	F T T T

vi

P Q R	R ↔ ~P ∨ (R & Q)
T T T	T F T T
T T F	T F F F
T F T	F F F F
T F F	T F F F
F T T	T T T T
F T F	F T T F
F F T	T T T F
F F F	F T T F

vii

P Q	(P & Q ↔ Q) → (Q → P)
T T	T T T T
T F	F T T T
F T	F F T F
F F	F T T T

viii

P Q	(P ↔ ~Q) ↔ (~P ↔ ~Q)
T T	F F F F T F
T F	T T F F F T
F T	T F F T F F
F F	F T F T T T

ix

P Q R   (P ↔ Q) ↔ (P ∨ R → (~Q → R))

P Q R							
T T T	T	T	T	T	F	T	
T T F	T	T	T	T	F	T	
T F T	F	F	T	T	T	T	
T F F	F	T	T	F	T	F	
F T T	F	F	T	T	F	T	
F T F	F	F	F	T	F	T	
F F T	T	T	T	T	T	T	
F F F	T	T	F	T	T	F	

x

P Q R S (P & Q) ∨ (R & S) → (P & R) ∨ (Q & S)

P Q R S							
T T T T	T	T	T	T	T	T	T
T T T F	T	T	F	T	T	T	F
T T F T	T	T	F	T	F	T	T
T T F F	T	T	F	F	F	F	F
T F T T	F	T	T	T	T	T	F
T F T F	F	F	F	T	T	T	F
T F F T	F	F	F	T	F	F	F
T F F F	F	F	F	T	F	F	F
F T T T	F	T	T	T	F	T	T
F T T F	F	F	F	T	F	F	F
F T F T	F	F	F	T	F	T	T
F T F F	F	F	F	T	F	F	F
F F T T	F	T	T	F	F	F	F
F F T F	F	F	F	T	F	F	F
F F F T	F	F	F	T	F	F	F
F F F F	F	F	F	T	F	F	F

Exercise 2.2

i		VALID	
1	(1)	P & ~Q A	
2	(2)	P ↔ Q	A [for RAA]
1	(3)	P	1 &E
1,2	(4)	Q	2,3 BP
1	(5)	~Q	1 &E
1	(6)	~(P ↔ Q)	4,5 RAA (2)

ii   INVALID
            P:T   Q:F   R:T

iii   INVALID
            P:T   Q:F   R:F

iv   VALID
1   (1)   P ∨ Q → R   A
2   (2)   P   A [for →I]
2   (3)   P ∨ Q   2 ∨I
1,2   (4)   R   1,3 →E
1   (5)   P → R   4 →I (2)

v   INVALID
            P:T   Q:T   R:F

vi   VALID
1   (1)   (P → ~P) → (~P → P)   A
2   (2)   ~P   A [for RAA]
2   (3)   P → ~P   2 TC
1,2   (4)   ~P → P   1,3 →E
1,2   (5)   P   2,4 →E
1   (6)   P   2,5 RAA (2)

vii   INVALID
            P:T   Q:F   R:T

viii   INVALID
            P:T   Q:F   R:T   S:F

ix   INVALID
            P:F   Q:F   R:F

x   INVALID
            P:T   Q:F   R:T   S:F

xi   VALID
1   (1)   P ∨ Q   A
2   (2)   P   A [for →I]
2   (3)   ~P → R   2 FA

	(4)	$P \rightarrow (\sim P \rightarrow R)$	3 $\rightarrow$I (2)
5	(5)	Q	A [for $\rightarrow$I]
5	(6)	$\sim Q \rightarrow R$	5 FA
	(7)	$Q \rightarrow (\sim Q \rightarrow R)$	6 $\rightarrow$I (5)
1	(8)	$(\sim P \rightarrow R) \vee (\sim Q \rightarrow R)$	1,4,7 Com Dil

xii   VALID

1	(1)	$P \leftrightarrow (R \rightarrow P \vee \sim Q)$	A
2	(2)	$\sim(R \rightarrow P \vee Q)$	A
3	(3)	Q	A [for RAA]
3	(4)	$P \vee Q$	3 $\vee$I
3	(5)	$R \rightarrow P \vee Q$	4 TC
2	(6)	$\sim Q$	2,5 RAA (3)

xiii   VALID

1	(1)	$\sim(R \,\&\, \sim P \rightarrow Q \vee R)$	A
2	(2)	$Q \leftrightarrow R$	A [for RAA]
1	(3)	$(R \,\&\, \sim P) \,\&\, \sim(Q \vee R)$	1 Neg$\rightarrow$
1	(4)	$R \,\&\, \sim P$	3 &E
1	(5)	R	4 &E
1,2	(6)	Q	2,5 BP
1,2	(7)	$Q \vee R$	6 $\vee$I
1	(8)	$\sim(Q \vee R)$	3 &E
1	(9)	$\sim(Q \leftrightarrow R)$	7,8 RAA (2)

xiv   VALID

1	(1)	$P \rightarrow (Q \,\&\, R \rightarrow S)$	A
2	(2)	P	A
3	(3)	$\sim S$	A
4	(4)	$Q \,\&\, R$	A [for RAA]
1,2	(5)	$Q \,\&\, R \rightarrow S$	1,2 $\rightarrow$E
1,2,4	(6)	S	4,5 $\rightarrow$E
1,2,3	(7)	$\sim(Q \,\&\, R)$	3,6 RAA (4)

xv   INVALID
       P:F   Q:F   R:T

xvi   INVALID
          P:T   Q:F   R:F   S:F   T:F

xvii   VALID
1   (1)   Q → (P → R & ~Q)   A
2   (2)   ~Q → ~(T ∨ V)   A
3   (3)   U & S ↔ P   A
4   (4)   ~(S → ~U)   A [for →I]
4   (5)   S & U   4 Neg→
4   (6)   U & S   5 Comm
3,4   (7)   P   3,6 BP
8   (8)   T   A [for RAA]
8   (9)   T ∨ V   8 ∨I
2,8   (10)   Q   2.9 MTT
1,2,8   (11)   P → R & ~Q   1,10 →E
1,2,3,4,8 (12)   R & ~Q   7,11 →E
1,2,3,4,8 (13)   ~Q   12 &E
1,2,3,4   (14)   ~T   10,13 RAA (8)
1,2,3   (15)   ~(S → U) → ~T   14 →I (4)
1,2,3   (16)   (S → ~U) ∨ ~T   15 ∨→

xviii   INVALID
          P:T   Q:F   R:F   S:F   T:F   U:F   V:T   W:F

Exercise 2.4.2

i   P:F   Q:T
ii   P:T   Q:F
iii   P:T   Q:T   R:F
iv   P:F   Q:F   R:T
v   P:T   Q:F   R:T
vi   P:F   Q:F   R:F   S:T
vii   P:T   Q:F   R:T   S:F   T:T
viii   P:F   Q:F   R:T
ix   P:T   Q:T   R:F   S:T   T:F
x   P:T   Q:F   R:T   S:F
xi   P:T   Q:F   R:F   S:F   T:T
xii   P:F   Q:T   R:F   S:T   T:T
xiii   VALID
1   (1)   P → (~Q → ~R & ~S)   A

2	(2)	~(R ↔ S)	A
3	(3)	~Q	A
4	(4)	P	A
1,4	(5)	~Q → ~R & ~S	1,4 →E
1,3,4	(6)	~R & ~S	3,5 →E
1,3,4	(7)	~R	6 &E
1,3,4	(8)	~S	6 &E
1,3,4	(9)	R → S	7 FA
1,3,4	(10)	S → R	8 FA
1,3,4	(11)	R ↔ S	9,10 ↔I
1,2,3	(12)	~P	2,11 RAA (4)

xiv	P:F	Q:T	R:T	S:F	T:F
xv	P:T	Q:F	R:T	S:F	T:F	U:F
xvi	P:T	Q:F	R:T	S:F	
xvii	VALID				

1	(1)	~(P → ~Q & R)	A
2	(2)	~R ↔ ~P	A
1	(3)	P & ~(~Q & R)	1 Neg→
1	(4)	P	3 &E
1	(5)	~(~Q & R)	3 &E
1	(6)	~~Q ∨ ~R	5 DM
1,2	(7)	R	2,4 BT
1,2	(8)	~~Q	6,7 ∨E
1,2	(9)	Q	8 DN
1,2	(10)	P & Q	4,9 &I

xviii	VALID		
1	(1)	(P → Q) & (~Q → P & R) → (S ∨ T → ~Q)	A
2	(2)	Q	A
2	(3)	P → Q	2 TC
2	(4)	~Q → P & R	2 FA
2	(5)	(P → Q) & (~Q → P & R)	3,4 &I
1,2	(6)	S ∨ T → ~Q	1,5 →E
1,2	(7)	~(S ∨ T)	2,6 MTT
1,2	(8)	~S & ~T	7 DM
1,2	(9)	~(~S → T)	8 Neg→
1	(10)	Q → ~(~S → T)	9 →I (2)

xix		VALID		
1	(1)	P ∨ ~Q → ~P & ~Q		A [for →I]
2	(2)	P		A [for RAA]
2	(3)	P ∨ ~Q		2 ∨I
1,2	(4)	~P & ~Q		2,3 →E
1,2	(5)	~P		4 &E
1	(6)	~P		2,5 RAA(2)
	(7)	((P ∨ ~Q) → (~P & ~Q)) → ~P		6 →I(1)
8	(8)	~P		A [for →I]
9	(9)	P ∨ ~Q		A [for →I]
8,9	(10)	~Q		8,9 ∨E
8,9	(11)	~P & ~Q		8,10 &I
8	(12)	(P ∨ ~Q) → (~P & ~Q)		11 →I(9)
	(13)	~P → ((P ∨ ~Q) → (~P & ~Q))		12 →I(8)
	(14)	((P ∨ ~Q) → (~P & ~Q)) ↔ ~P		7,13 ↔I

xx		VALID		
1	(1)	Q ↔ ~Q		A
2	(2)	Q		A
1,2	(3)	~Q		1,2 BP
1	(4)	~Q		2,3 RAA (2)
1	(5)	Q		1,4 BP
1	(6)	Q ∨ (P ↔ ~P)		5 ∨I
1	(7)	P ↔ ~P		4,6 ∨E

Chapter 3

Exercise 3.1.1

i	Not a wff
ii	Not a wff
iii	Universal
iv	Existential
v	Not a wff
vi	Not a wff
vii	Universal
viii	Not a wff (but acceptable biconditional abbreviation given the parenthesis-dropping convention)

ix   Negation
x   Not a wff (but acceptable conditional abbreviation given the parenthesis-dropping convention)
xi   Not a wff (but acceptable conditional abbreviation given the parenthesis-dropping convention)
xii   Negation
xiii   Not a wff
xiv   Existential
xv   Not a wff
xvi   Atomic sentence
xvii   Not a wff
xviii   Not a wff
xix   Not a wff
xx   Universal
xxi   Not a wff
xxii   Not a wff
xxiii   Negation
xxiv   Biconditional
xxx   Not a wff

Exercise 3.1.2

	Open Formula	*Example WFF*
i	Fz	$\exists z Fz$
ii	None	
iii	Gcax	
iv	Gxy	
	Gyx	
	(Gxy & Gyx)	
	$\forall y (Gxy\ \&\ Gyx)$	
v	Gxy	$\exists y \sim \forall x Gxy$
	Hy	$\sim \forall y \sim Hy$
vi	Ax	$\forall x Ax$
	Fxx	$\exists x Fxx$
vii	Fxy	
	Hxyz	
	Jz	
	(Hxyz & Jz)	
	$\forall z (Hxyz\ \&\ Jz)$	
	$(Fxy \rightarrow \forall z(Hxyz\ \&\ Jz))$	
	$\forall y (Fxy \rightarrow \forall z(Hxyz\ \&\ Jz))$	

viii	Fxx
	Fxy
	∀yFxy
ix	Hz
	Jx
	(Hz ∨ Jx)
	∃z(Hz ∨ Jx)
	~∃z(Hz ∨ Jx)
x	Fxx
	(Ha ∨ Fxx)
	~(Ha ∨ Fxx)
xi	None
xii	Fx
xiii	Fx ∀xFx
xiv	Fyyy
	(Fyyy & P)
xv	Fzx
	Hxyz
	(Fzy ↔ Hxyz)

Exercise 3.2

Translation scheme is provided only where it is not obvious.

  alt: indicates an alternative, logically equivalent translation.
  amb: indicates non-equivalent rendering of an ambiguous sentence.
  inc!   indicates a common, but incorrect answer.

1	∀x(Dx → Mx)
inc!	∀x(Dx & Mx)
2	∃x(Sx & Ox)
inc!	∃x(Sx → Ox)
3	∀x(Fx → ~Ex)
alt:	~∃x(Fx & Ex)
inc!	~∀x(Fx → Ex)
4	~∀x(Fx → Px)
alt:	∃x(Fx & ~Px)
5	∀x(Rx → ~Ex) & ∀x(Ax → ~Ex)
alt:	∀x(Rx ∨ Ax → ~Ex)
inc!	∀x(Rx & Ax → ~Ex)

6	∃x(Px & Ax) & ∃x(Rx & Ax)
inc!	∃x((Px & Rx) & Ax)
inc!	∃x((Px ∨ Rx) & Ax)
7	∀x(Gx → Lx)
inc!	∀x(Lx → Gx)
8	∀x(Sx → (Px → Tx ∨ Bx))
alt:	∀x(Sx & Px → Tx ∨ Bx)
9	∀x(Mx ↔ Px)
alt:	∀x((Mx → Px) & (Px → Mx))
10	∀x(Fx → ~Wx ∨ Ex)
alt:	∀x(Fx & Wx → Ex)
11	(∃x(Ox & Cx) & ∃x(Ox & Mx)) & ~∃x(Cx & Mx)
12	∀x(Ix → Px)
alt:	∀x(~Px → ~Ix)
inc!	∀x(Px → Ix)
13	∀x(Ax → (~Wx → Nx))
14	∀x(Ax → (Nx → ~Wx))
15	∃x(Sx & (Px & Fx)) & ~∀x(Px & Fx → Sx)
alt:	∃x(Sx & (Px & Fx)) & ∃x((Px & Fx) & ~Sx)
16	Wa & ∀x(Wx → Mx) → Ma
17	∀x(Sx → (~Nx ∨ Mx))
18	∀x(Ox & Ex → ~Px)
alt:	~∃x((Ox & Ex) & Px)
19	∀x(Px → ~Hx)
amb:	~∀x(Px → Hx) [possible reading in some regional dialects of English]
20	~∀x(Px → Cx)
21	∀x(Mx & Wx → Bx)
22	∃x((Mx & Wx) & Fx)

23-29	Translation scheme I using single-place predicates only:
	Tα: α is a trick
	Wα: α is a whale
	Sα: Shamu can do α
	Cα: α can do a trick
	s: Shamu

Note: Strictly we should use a letter from a-d for a name, but the use of s for Shamu is more perspicuous.

23        $\forall x(Tx \rightarrow Sx)$
24        $\forall x(Tx \rightarrow Sx)$
25        $\sim\forall x(Tx \rightarrow Sx)$
26        $\forall x(Tx \rightarrow \sim Sx)$
alternative translation that is not logically equivalent: $\sim Cs$
27        $\exists x(Wx \ \& \ Cx) \rightarrow Cs$
          $\forall x(Wx \ \& \ Cx \rightarrow Cs)$ Note difference in scope.
amb i: $\forall x(Wx \rightarrow Cx) \rightarrow Cs$ Less natural reading.
amb ii: If any whale can do a trick, Shamu can do that same trick.
This reading is not expressible using single-place predicates only.
28        $\forall x(Wx \rightarrow Cx) \rightarrow Cs$ Note scope again.
29        $\exists x(Wx \ \& \ Cx) \rightarrow \forall x(Wx \rightarrow Cx)$
amb $\forall x(Wx \rightarrow Cx) \rightarrow \forall x(Wx \rightarrow Cx)$ This reading is less natural.

23-29   Translation Scheme II using many-place predicates
          $T\alpha$: α is a trick
          $C\alpha\beta$: α can do β
          $W\alpha$: α is a whale
          s: Shamu

23        $\forall x(Tx \rightarrow Csx)$
24        $\forall x(Tx \rightarrow Csx)$
25        $\sim\forall x(Tx \rightarrow Csx)$
alt: $\exists x(Tx \ \& \ \sim Csx)$
26        $\forall x(Tx \rightarrow \sim Csx)$
27        $\exists xy((Wx \ \& \ Ty) \ \& \ Cxy) \rightarrow \exists z(Tz \ \& \ Csz)$
alt: $\forall xy(((Wx \ \& \ Ty) \ \& \ Cxy) \rightarrow \exists z(Tz \ \& \ Csz))$ Scope!
amb-i: $\forall x\exists y(Wx \rightarrow Ty \ \& \ Cxy) \rightarrow \exists z(Tz \ \& \ Csz)$
amb-ii: $\forall xy(((Wx \ \& Ty) \ \& \ Cxy) \rightarrow Csy)$
This is the ambiguous reading not expressible with the previous translation scheme.
28        $\forall x\exists y(Wx \rightarrow (Ty \ \& \ Cxy)) \rightarrow \exists z(Tz \ \& \ Csz)$
alt: $\forall x(Wx \rightarrow \exists y(Ty \ \& \ Cxy)) \rightarrow \exists z(Tz \ \& \ Csz)$
29        $\exists xy((Wx \ \& \ Ty) \ \& \ Cxy) \rightarrow \forall x(Wx \rightarrow \exists y(Ty \ \& \ Cxy))$
amb: $\forall x\exists y(Wx \rightarrow (Ty \ \& \ Cxy)) \rightarrow \forall x(Wx \rightarrow \exists y(Ty \ \& \ Cxy))$

30   Agb
31        $\exists x Axb$

32   ∃xAgx

33   ∀xAbx

34   ∀xAxb

35   ∃xyAxy

36   ∃x∀yAxy

  amb: ∀y∃xAxy

37   ∀x∃yAxy

  amb: ∃y∀xAxy

38   ∀xyAxy

39   ∀xAxx

40   ∃xAxx

41   ∀x~Axx

  alt: ~∃xAxx

42   ∃x∀y~Axy

  alt: ∃x~∃yAxy

Translation Scheme for 43-46.

Sαβγ: α said β to γ

Pα: α is a person

43   ∀x(Px → ∃y∀z(Pz → Sxyz))

  amb: ∀xy(Px & Py → ∃zSxzy))

44   ∀x(Px → ∃yz(Pz & Sxyz))

45   ∀x(Px → ∃y(Py & ~∃zSxzy))

46   ∀xy(Px & Py → ~∃zSxzy)

47   ∃xyz((Rx & (Cy & Sxy)) & (Dz & Lxz))

48   ∃x(Fx & ∀y(Hy → Sxy))

  alt: ∃x∀y(Fx & (Hy → Sxy))

  amb: ∃x(Fx & ∃y(Hy & Sxy))

49   ∃x(Fx & ∀y(My → Sxy))

50   ∃x(Wx & ∀y(Fy & Exy → My))

  amb: ∃x(Wx & ∀y(Exy → Fy & My))

51   ∃x(Wx & ∀y(Fy & My → ~Exy))

52   ∃xy((My & Fy) & Exy) → ∀x(Sx → ∃y((My & Fy) & Exy))

  amb: ∃xy((My & Fy) & Exy) → ∃x(Sx & ∃y((My & Fy) & Exy))

53   ∀wxyz((Jw & Txw) & (Oy & Tzy) → Lxz) [Tαβ: α is β's tail]

-- alt: ∀wxyz(((Jw & Tx) & Bxw) & ((Oy & Tz) & Bzy) → Lxz) [Bαβ: α belongs
           to β]

54   ∀x(∃y(Cy & Sxy) → Ax)

 alt: ∀xy(Cy & Sxy → Ax)

55   ∀uvxy(Bu & Pvu → (Hx & Pyx → Mvy)) &

           ∀uvwx(Ou & Evu → ((Mw ∨ Bw) & Exw → Avx & ~Mvx))

56   Ambiguous.

           i. The amount eaten by some whales is more than the amount eaten by any
           fish.

           Translation scheme:

           Aα: α is an amount (of food)

           Fα: α is a fish

           Eαβ: α eats β amount (of food)

           Gαβ: α is greater than β

           ∃x(Wx & ∃y((Ay & Exy) & ∀zw(Fz & Aw & Ezw → Gyw)))

           ii. The amount eaten by some whales is more than the amount eaten by all
           the fishes combined.

           Addition to translation scheme.

           a: the amount eaten by all the fishes combined

           ∃xy((Wx & Ay) & (Exy & Gya))

57   ∃x(Mx & ∀y(My → (Gxy ↔ ~Gyy)))

(Using identity)

58   ∃x(Cx & ∀y(Cy → y=x))

59   ∃x x=p

 alt: ∃x(x=p & ∀y(y=p → y=x))

60   ∃xy(((Tx & Ty) & x ≠ y) & (Ebx & Eby))

61   ∀x(x≠b → Exb) & ~Ebb

62   ∀x(Dx → ∃y((Ty & Byx) & ∀z(Tz & Bzx → y=z))

Exercise 3.3.1

i is an instance of v

ii is an instance of vi

ii is an instance ix

iv is an instance of i
iv is an instance of iii
x is an instance of ii

Exercise 3.3.2

S87		$\exists x(Gx \, \& \sim Fx), \forall x(Gx \rightarrow Hx) \vdash \exists x(Hx \, \& \sim Fx)$	
1	(1)	$\exists x(Gx \, \& \sim Fx)$	A
2	(2)	$\forall x(Gx \rightarrow Hx)$	A
2	(3)	$Ga \rightarrow Ha$	2 $\forall$E
4	(4)	$Ga \, \& \sim Fa$	A [for $\exists$E on 1]
4	(5)	Ga	4 &E
2,4	(6)	Ha	3,5 $\rightarrow$E
4	(7)	$\sim Fa$	4 &E
2,4	(8)	$Ha \, \& \sim Fa$	6,7 &I
2,4	(9)	$\exists x(Hx \, \& \sim Fx)$	8 $\exists$I
1,2	(10)	$\exists x(Hx \, \& \sim Fx)$	1,9 $\exists$E (4)

S88		$\exists x(Gx \, \& \, Fx), \forall x(Fx \rightarrow \sim Hx) \vdash \exists x \sim Hx$	
1	(1)	$\exists x(Gx \, \& \, Fx)$	A
2	(2)	$\forall x(Fx \rightarrow \sim Hx)$	A
2	(3)	$Fa \rightarrow \sim Ha$	2 $\forall$E
4	(4)	$Ga \, \& \, Fa$	A [for $\exists$E on 1]
4	(5)	Ga	4 &E
4	(6)	Fa	4 &E
2,4	(7)	$\sim Ha$	3,6 $\rightarrow$E
2,4	(8)	$\exists x \sim Hx$	7 $\exists$I
1,2	(9)	$\exists x \sim Hx$	1,8 $\exists$E (4)

S89		$\forall x(Gx \rightarrow \sim Fx), \forall x(\sim Fx \rightarrow \sim Hx) \vdash \forall x(Gx \rightarrow \sim Hx)$	
1	(1)	$\forall x(Gx \rightarrow \sim Fx)$	A
2	(2)	$\forall x(\sim Fx \rightarrow \sim Hx)$	A
1	(3)	$Ga \rightarrow \sim Fa$	1 $\forall$E
2	(4)	$\sim Fa \rightarrow \sim Ha$	2 $\forall$E
1,2	(5)	$Ga \rightarrow \sim Ha$	3,4 HS
1,2	(6)	$\forall x(Gx \rightarrow \sim Hx)$	5 $\forall$I

S91 $\forall x(Gx \rightarrow \exists y(Fy \& Hy)) \vdash \forall x \sim Fx \rightarrow \sim \exists z Gz$

1	(1)	$\forall x(Gx \rightarrow \exists y(Fy \& Hy))$	A
1	(2)	$Ga \rightarrow \exists y(Fy \& Hy)$	1 $\forall$E
3	(3)	$\forall x \sim Fx$	A [for $\rightarrow$I]
3	(4)	$\sim Fa$	3 $\forall$E
5	(5)	$\exists z Gz$	A [for RAA]
6	(6)	Ga	A [for $\exists$E on 5]
1,6	(7)	$\exists y(Fy \& Hy)$	2,6 $\rightarrow$E
8	(8)	$Fa \& Ha$	A [for $\exists$E on 7]
8	(9)	Fa	8 &E
3,8	(10)	$\sim \exists z Gz$	4,9 RAA (5)
1,3,6	(11)	$\sim \exists z Gz$	7,10 $\exists$E (8)
1,3,5	(12)	$\sim \exists z Gz$	5,11 $\exists$E (6)
1,3	(13)	$\sim \exists z Gz$	5,12 RAA (5)
1	(14)	$\forall x \sim Fx \rightarrow \sim \exists z Gz$	13 $\rightarrow$I (3)

S92 $\forall x(Gx \rightarrow Hx \& Jx), \forall x(Fx \lor \sim Jx \rightarrow Gx) \vdash \forall x(Fx \rightarrow Hx)$

1	(1)	$\forall x(Gx \rightarrow Hx \& Jx)$	A
2	(2)	$\forall x(Fx \lor \sim Jx \rightarrow Gx)$	A
1	(3)	$Ga \rightarrow Ha \& Ja$	1 $\forall$E
2	(4)	$Fa \lor \sim Ja \rightarrow Ga$	2 $\forall$E
5	(5)	Fa	A [for $\rightarrow$I]
5	(6)	$Fa \lor \sim Ja$	5 $\lor$I
2,5	(7)	Ga	4,6 $\rightarrow$E
1,2,5	(8)	$Ha \& Ja$	3,7 $\rightarrow$E
1,2,5	(9)	Ha	8 &E
1,2	(10)	$Fa \rightarrow Ha$	9 $\rightarrow$I (5)
1,2	(11)	$\forall x(Fx \rightarrow Hx)$	10 $\forall$I

S93 $\forall x(Gx \& Kx \leftrightarrow Hx), \sim \exists x(Fx \& Gx) \vdash \forall x \sim(Fx \& Hx)$

1	(1)	$\forall x(Gx \& Kx \leftrightarrow Hx)$	A
2	(2)	$\sim \exists x(Fx \& Gx)$	A
3	(3)	$Fa \& Ha$	A [for RAA]
1	(4)	$Ga \& Ka \leftrightarrow Ha$	1 $\forall$E
3	(5)	Ha	3 &E
1,3	(6)	$Ga \& Ka$	4,5 BP
1,3	(7)	Ga	6 &E

3	(8)	Fa	3 &E
1,3	(9)	Fa & Ga	7,8 &I
1,3	(10)	∃x(Fx & Gx)	9 ∃I
1,2	(11)	~(Fa & Ha)	2,10 RAA (3)
1,2	(12)	∀x~(Fx & Hx)	11 ∀I

S95   ∀x(~Gx ∨ ~Hx), ∀x((Jx → Fx) → Hx) ⊢ ~∃x(Fx & Gx)

1	(1)	∀x(~Gx ∨ ~Hx)	A
2	(2)	∀x((Jx → Fx) → Hx)	A
3	(3)	∃x(Fx & Gx)	A [for RAA]
4	(4)	Fa & Ga	A [for ∃E on 3]
4	(5)	Fa	4 &E
4	(6)	Ga	4 &E
1	(7)	~Ga ∨ ~Ha	1 ∀E
1,4	(8)	~Ha	6,7 ∨E
4	(9)	Ja → Fa	5 TC
2	(10)	(Ja → Fa) → Ha	2 ∀E
2,4	(11)	Ha	9,10 →E
1,2,4	(12)	~∃x(Fx & Gx)	8,11 RAA (3)
1,2,3	(13)	~∃x(Fx & Gx)	3,12 ∃E (4)
1,2	(14)	~∃x(Fx & Gx)	3,13 RAA (3)

S96   ~∃x(~Gx & Hx), ∀x(Fx → ~Hx) ⊢ ∀x(Fx ∨ ~Gx → ~Hx)

1	(1)	~∃x(~Gx & Hx) A	
2	(2)	∀x(Fx → ~Hx)	A
2	(3)	Fa → ~Ha	2 ∀E
4	(4)	Fa ∨ ~Ga	A [for →I]
5	(5)	~(~Ga → ~Ha)	A [for RAA]
5	(6)	~Ga & Ha	5 Neg→
5	(7)	∃x(~Gx & Hx)	6 ∃I
1	(8)	~Ga → ~Ha	1,7 RAA (5)
1,2,4	(9)	~Ha	3,4,8 Sim Dil
1,2	(10)	Fa ∨ ~Ga → ~Ha	9 →I (4)
1,2	(11)	∀x(Fx ∨ ~Gx → ~Hx)	10 ∀I

S101   ∀x(Fx ↔ Gx) ⊢ ∀xFx ↔ ∀xGx

| 1 | (1) | ∀x(Fx ↔ Gx) | A |

2	(2)	∀xFx	A [for →I]
2	(3)	Fa	2 ∀E
1	(4)	Fa ↔ Ga	1 ∀E
1,2	(5)	Ga	3,4 BP
1,2	(6)	∀xGx	5 ∀I
1	(7)	∀xFx → ∀xGx	6 →I (2)
8	(8)	∀xGx	A [for →I]
8	(9)	Ga	8 ∀E
1,8	(10)	Fa	4,9 BP
1,8	(11)	∀xFx	10 ∀I
1	(12)	∀xGx → ∀xFx	11 →I (8)
1	(13)	∀xFx ↔ ∀xGx	7,12 ↔I

S102   ∃xFx → ∀y(Gy → Hy), ∃xJx → ∃xGx ⊢ ∃x(Fx & Jx) → ∃zHz

1	(1)	∃xFx → ∀y(Gy → Hy)	A
2	(2)	∃xJx → ∃xGx	A
3	(3)	∃x(Fx & Jx)	A [for →I]
4	(4)	Fa & Ja	A [for ∃E on 3]
4	(5)	Fa	4 &E
4	(6)	Ja	4 &E
4	(7)	∃xFx	5 ∃I
4	(8)	∃xJx	6 ∃I
1,4	(9)	∀y(Gy → Hy)	1,7 →E
2,4	(10)	∃xGx	2,8 →E
11	(11)	Gb	A [for ∃E on 10]
1,4	(12)	Gb → Hb	9 ∀E
1,4,11	(13)	Hb	11,12 →E
1,4,11	(14)	∃zHz	13 ∃I
1,2,4	(15)	∃zHz	10,14 ∃E (11)
1,2,3	(16)	∃zHz	3,15 ∃E (4)
1,2	(17)	∃x(Fx & Jx) → ∃zHz	16 →I (3)

S105   ∀x(Fx ∨ Hx → Gx & Kx), ~∀x(Kx & Gx) ⊢ ∃x~Hx

1	(1)	∀x(Fx ∨ Hx → Gx & Kx)	A
2	(2)	~∀x(Kx & Gx)	A
1	(3)	Fa ∨ Ha → Ga & Ka	1 ∀E
4	(4)	~∃x~Hx	A [for RAA]

5	(5)	~Ha	A
5	(6)	∃x~Hx	5 ∃I
4	(7)	Ha	4,6 RAA (5)
4	(8)	Fa ∨ Ha	7 ∨I
1,4	(9)	Ga & Ka	3,8 →E
1,4	(10)	Ka & Ga	9 Comm
1,4	(11)	∀x(Kx & Gx)	10 ∀I
1,2	(12)	∃x~Hx	2,11 RAA (4)

S107		∀x(Fx ↔ ∀yGy) ⊢ ∀xFx ∨ ∀x~Fx	
1	(1)	∀x(Fx ↔ ∀yGy)	A
2	(2)	~∀xFx	A [for →I]
3	(3)	~∃x~Fx	A [for RAA]
4	(4)	~Fa	A
4	(5)	∃x~Fx	4 ∃I
3	(6)	Fa	3,5 RAA (4)
3	(7)	∀xFx	6 ∀I
2	(8)	∃x~Fx	2,7 RAA (3)
9	(9)	~Fa	A [for ∃E on 8]
1	(10)	Fa ↔ ∀yGy	1 ∀E
1,9	(11)	~∀yGy	9,10 BT
1,2	(12)	~∀yGy	8,11 ∃E (9)
13	(13)	∃xFx	A [for RAA]
14	(14)	Fa	A [for ∃E on 13]
1,14	(15)	∀yGy	10,14 BP
1,13	(16)	∀yGy	13,15 ∃E (14)
1,2	(17)	~∃xFx	12,16 RAA (13)
19	(18)	Fa	A [for RAA]
19	(19)	∃xFx	18 ∃I
1,2	(20)	~Fa	17,19 RAA (18)
1,2	(21)	∀x~Fx	20 ∀I
1	(22)	~∀xFx → ∀x~Fx	21 →I (2)
1	(23)	∀xFx ∨ ∀x~Fx	22 ∨→

S109		∀x(Dx → Fx) ⊢ ∀z(Dz → (∀y(Fy → Gy) → Gz))	
1	(1)	∀x(Dx → Fx)	A
2	(2)	Da	A

3	(3)	$\forall y(Fy \rightarrow Gy)$	A
1	(4)	$Da \rightarrow Fa$	1 $\forall$E
3	(5)	$Fa \rightarrow Ga$	3 $\forall$E
1,3	(6)	$Da \rightarrow Ga$	4,5 HS
1,2,3	(7)	Ga	2,6 $\rightarrow$E
1,2	(8)	$\forall y(Fy \rightarrow Gy) \rightarrow Ga$	7 $\rightarrow$I (3)
1	(9)	$Da \rightarrow (\forall y(Fy \rightarrow Gy) \rightarrow Ga)$	8 $\rightarrow$I (2)
1	(10)	$\forall z(Dz \rightarrow (\forall y(Fy \rightarrow Gy) \rightarrow Gz))$	9 $\forall$I

S111		$\forall xFx \vdash \sim\exists xGx \leftrightarrow \sim(\exists x(Fx \;\&\; Gx) \;\&\; \forall y(Gy \rightarrow Fy))$	
1	(1)	$\forall xFx$	A
2	(2)	$\sim\exists xGx$	A [for $\rightarrow$I]
3	(3)	$\exists x(Fx \;\&\; Gx) \;\&\; \forall y(Gy \rightarrow Fy)$	A [for RAA]
3	(4)	$\exists x(Fx \;\&\; Gx)$	3 &E
5	(5)	$Fa \;\&\; Ga$	A [for $\exists$E on 4]
5	(6)	Ga	5 &E
5	(7)	$\exists xGx$	6 $\exists$I
3	(8)	$\exists xGx$	4,7 $\exists$E (5)
2	(9)	$\sim(\exists x(Fx \;\&\; Gx) \;\&\; \forall y(Gy \rightarrow Fy))$	2,8 RAA (3)
	(10)	$\sim\exists xGx \rightarrow \sim(\exists x(Fx \;\&\; Gx) \;\&\; \forall y(Gy \rightarrow Fy))$	9 $\rightarrow$I (2)
11	(11)	$\exists xGx$	A [for $\rightarrow$I]
12	(12)	Ga	A [for $\exists$E on 11]
1	(13)	Fa	1 $\forall$E
1	(14)	$Ga \rightarrow Fa$	13 TC
1	(15)	$\forall x(Gx \rightarrow Fx)$	14 $\forall$I
1,12	(16)	$Fa \;\&\; Ga$	12,13 &I
1,12	(17)	$\exists x(Fx \;\&\; Gx)$	16 $\exists$I
1,12	(18)	$\exists x(Fx \;\&\; Gx) \;\&\; \forall x(Gx \rightarrow Fx)$	15,17 &I
1,11	(19)	$\exists x(Fx \;\&\; Gx) \;\&\; \forall x(Gx \rightarrow Fx)$	11,18 $\exists$E (12)
1	(20)	$\exists xGx \rightarrow \exists x(Fx \;\&\; Gx) \;\&\; \forall x(Gx \rightarrow Fx)$	19 $\rightarrow$I (11)
1	(21)	$\sim(\exists x(Fx \;\&\; Gx) \;\&\; \forall x(Gx \rightarrow Fx)) \rightarrow \sim\exists xGx$	20 Trans
1	(22)	$\sim\exists xGx \leftrightarrow \sim(\exists x(Fx \;\&\; Gx) \;\&\; \forall y(Gy \rightarrow Fy))$	10,21 $\leftrightarrow$I

S112		$\forall x(\exists yFyx \rightarrow \forall zFxz) \vdash \forall yx(Fyx \rightarrow Fxy)$	
1	(1)	$\forall x(\exists yFyx \rightarrow \forall zFxz)$	A
2	(2)	Fab	A [for $\rightarrow$I]
2	(3)	$\exists yFyb$	2 $\exists$I

1	(4)	∃yFyb → ∀zFbz	1 ∀E
1,2	(5)	∀zFbz	3,4 →E
1,2	(6)	Fba	5 ∀E
1	(7)	Fab → Fba	6 →I (2)
1	(8)	∀x(Fax → Fxa)	7 ∀I
1	(9)	∀yx(Fyx → Fxy)	8 ∀I

S116

1	(1)	∀xy(Fxy → ~Fyx)	A
1	(2)	∀y(Fby → ~Fyb)	1 ∀E
1	(3)	(Fbb → ~Fbb)	2 ∀E
4	(4)	∃xFxx	A [for RAA]
5	(5)	Fbb	A [for ∃E]
1,5	(6)	~Fbb	3,5 →E
1,5	(7)	~∃xFxx	5,6 RAA (4)
1,4	(8)	~∃xFxx	4,7 ∃E (5)
1	(9)	~∃xFxx	4,8 RAA (4)

S123   a=b, b≠c ⊢ a≠c

1	(1)	a=b	A
2	(2)	b≠c	A
3	(3)	a=c	A [for RAA]
1,3	(4)	b=c	1,3 =E
1,2	(5)	a≠c	2,4 RAA (3)

S125*   ∀x x=x → ∃xFx, ∀x(~Fx ∨ Gx) ⊢ ∃x(Fx & Gx)

1	(1)	∀x x=x → ∃xFx	A
2	(2)	∀x(~Fx ∨ Gx)	A
	(3)	a=a	=I
	(4)	∀x x=x	3 ∀I
1	(5)	∃xFx	1,4 →E
6	(6)	Fa	A
2	(7)	~Fa ∨ Ga	2 ∀E
2,6	(8)	Ga	6,7 ∨E
2,6	(9)	Fa & Ga	6,8 &I
2,6	(10)	∃x(Fx & Gx)	9 ∃I
1,2	(11)	∃x(Fx & Gx)	5,10 ∃E (6)

S127* $\exists x((Fx \, \& \, \forall y(Fy \to y=x)) \, \& \, Gx), \sim Ga \vdash \sim Fa$

1	(1)	$\exists x((Fx \, \& \, \forall y(Fy \to y=x)) \, \& \, Gx)$	A
2	(2)	$\sim Ga$	A
3	(3)	$(Fb \, \& \, \forall y(Fy \to y=b)) \, \& \, Gb$	A
3	(4)	$Fb \, \& \, \forall y(Fy \to y=b)$	3 &E
3	(5)	$\forall y(Fy \to y=b)$	4 &E
6	(6)	Fa	A
3	(7)	$Fa \to a=b$	5 $\forall$E
3,6	(8)	$a=b$	6,7 $\to$E
3	(9)	Gb	3 &E
3,6	(10)	Ga	8,9 =E
2,3	(11)	$\sim Fa$	2,10 RAA (6)
1,2	(12)	$\sim Fa$	1,11 $\exists$E(3)

S130* $\forall x \exists y Gyx, \forall xy(Gxy \to \sim Gyx) \vdash \sim \exists y \forall x(x \neq y \to Gyx)$

1	(1)	$\forall x \exists y Gyx$	A
2	(2)	$\forall xy(Gxy \to \sim Gyx)$	A
3	(3)	$\exists y \forall x(x \neq y \to Gyx)$	A [for R$\Lambda\Lambda$]
4	(4)	$\forall x(x \neq a \to Gax)$	A [for $\exists$E]
1	(5)	$\exists y Gya$	1$\forall$E
6	(6)	Gba	A [for $\exists$E]
2	(7)	$\forall y(Gay \to \sim Gya)$	2 $\forall$E
2	(8)	$Gab \to \sim Gba$	7 $\forall$E
2,6	(9)	$\sim Gab$	6,8 $\to$E
4	(10)	$b \neq a \to Gab$	4 $\forall$E
2,4,6	(11)	$b=a$	9,10 MTT
2,4,6	(12)	Gaa	6,11=E
2,4,6	(13)	$\sim Gaa$	9,11=E
2,4,6	(14)	$\sim \exists y \forall x(x \neq y \to Gyx)$	12,13 RAA (3)
1,2,4	(15)	$\sim \exists y \forall x(x \neq y \to Gyx)$	5,14 $\exists$E (6)
1,2,3	(16)	$\sim \exists y \forall x(x \neq y \to Gyx)$	3,15 $\exists$E (4)
1,2	(17)	$\sim \exists y \forall x(x \neq y \to Gyx)$	3,16 RAA (3)

Exercise 3.4.1

S150   ~∀xPx ⊣⊢ ∃x~Px

(a)   ~∀xPx ⊢ ∃x~Px
1   (1)   ~∀xPx   A
2   (2)   ~∃x~Px   A
3   (3)   ~Pa   A
3   (4)   ∃x~Px   3 ∃I
2   (5)   Pa   2,4 RAA (3)
2   (6)   ∀xPx   5 ∀I
1   (7)   ∃x~Px   1,6 RAA (2)

(b)   ∃x~Px ⊢ ~∀xPx
1   (1)   ∃x~Px   A
2   (2)   ∀xPx   A
3   (3)   ~Pa   A
2   (4)   Pa   2 ∀E
3   (5)   ~∀xPx   3,4 RAA (2)
1   (6)   ~∀xPx   1,5 ∃E (3)

S155   ∀x(Px → Q) ⊣⊢ ∃xPx → Q

(a)   ∀x(Px → Q) ⊢ ∃xPx → Q
1   (1)   ∀x(Px → Q)   A
2   (2)   ∃xPx   A
1   (3)   Pa → Q   1 ∀E
4   (4)   Pa   A
1,4   (5)   Q   3,4 →E
1,2   (6)   Q   2,5 ∃E (4)
1   (7)   ∃xPx → Q   6 →I (2)

(b)   ∃xPx → Q ⊢ ∀x(Px → Q)
1   (1)   ∃xPx → Q   A
2   (2)   Pa   A
2   (3)   ∃xPx   2 ∃I

1,2	(4)	Q	1,3 →E
1	(5)	Pa → Q	4 →I (2)
1	(6)	∀x(Px → Q)	5 ∀I

S156   ∀xPx ∨ ∀xQx ⊢ ∀x(Px ∨ Qx)

1	(1)	∀xPx ∨ ∀xQx	A
2	(2)	∀xPx	A
2	(3)	Pa	2 ∀E
2	(4)	Pa ∨ Qa	3 ∨I
2	(5)	∀x(Px ∨ Qx)	4 ∀I
	(6)	∀xPx → ∀x(Px ∨ Qx)	5 →I (2)
7	(7)	∀xQx	A
7	(8)	Qa	7 ∀E
7	(9)	Pa ∨ Qa	8 ∨I
7	(10)	∀x(Px ∨ Qx)	9 ∀I
	(11)	∀xQx → ∀x(Px ∨ Qx)	10 →I (7)
1	(12)	∀x(Px ∨ Qx)	1,6,11 Sim Dil

S157   ∃xy(Px & Qy) ⊣⊢ ∃xPx & ∃xQx

(a)   ∃xy(Px & Qy) ⊢ ∃xPx & ∃xQx

1	(1)	∃xy(Px & Qy)	A
2	(2)	∃y(Pa & Qy)	A
3	(3)	Pa & Qb	A
3	(4)	Pa	3 &E
3	(5)	Qb	3 &E
3	(6)	∃xPx	4 ∃I
3	(7)	∃xQx	5 ∃I
3	(8)	∃xPx & ∃xQx	6,7 &I
2	(9)	∃xPx & ∃xQx	2,8 ∃E (3)
1	(10)	∃xPx & ∃xQx	1,9 ∃E (2)

(b)   ∃xPx & ∃xQx ⊢ ∃xy(Px & Qy)

1	(1)	∃xPx & ∃xQx	A
1	(2)	∃xPx	1 &E
1	(3)	∃xQx	1 &E
4	(4)	Pa	A

5	(5)	Qb	A
4,5	(6)	Pa & Qb	4,5 &I
4,5	(7)	∃y(Pa & Qy)	6 ∃I
4,5	(8)	∃xy(Px & Qy)	7 ∃I
1,4	(9)	∃xy(Px & Qy)	3,8 ∃E (5)
1	(10)	∃xy(Px & Qy)	2,9 ∃E (4)

S160   P → ∃xQx ⊣⊢ ∃x(P → Qx)

(a)   P → ∃xQx ⊢ ∃x(P → Qx)

1	(1)	P → ∃xQx	A
2	(2)	~∃x(P → Qx)	A
3	(3)	P → Qa	A
3	(4)	∃x(P → Qx)	3 ∃I
2	(5)	~(P → Qa)	2,4 RAA (3)
2	(6)	P & ~Qa	5 Neg→
2	(7)	P	6 &E
1,2	(8)	∃xQx	1,7 →E
2	(9)	~Qa	6 &E
10	(10)	Qa	A
10	(11)	∃x(P → Qx)	9,10 RAA (2)
1,2	(12)	∃x(P → Qx)	8,11 ∃E (10)
1	(13)	∃x(P → Qx)	2,12 RAA (2)

(b)   ∃x(P → Qx) ⊢ P → ∃xQx

1	(1)	∃x(P → Qx)	A
2	(2)	P	A
3	(3)	P → Qa	A
2,3	(4)	Qa	2,3 →E
2,3	(5)	∃xQx	4 ∃I
3	(6)	P → ∃xQx	5 →I (2)
1	(7)	P → ∃xQx	1,6 ∃E (3)

Exercise 3.4.2

T40   ⊢ ∀x(Fx → Gx) → (∀xFx → ∀xGx)

1	(1)	∀x(Fx → Gx)	A [for →I]
2	(2)	∀xFx	A [for →I]

1	(3)	Fa → Ga	1 ∀E
2	(4)	Fa	2 ∀E
1,2	(5)	Ga	3,4 →E
1,2	(6)	∀xGx	5 ∀I
1	(7)	∀xFx → ∀xGx	6 →I (2)
	(8)	∀x(Fx → Gx) → (∀xFx → ∀xGx)	7 →I (1)

T42		⊢ ∃x(Fx ∨ Gx) ↔ ∃xFx ∨ ∃xGx	
1	(1)	∃x(Fx ∨ Gx)	A [for →I]
2	(2)	~(∃xFx ∨ ∃xGx)	A [for RAA]
2	(3)	~∃xFx & ~∃xGx	2 DM
2	(4)	~∃xFx	3 &E
2	(5)	~∃xGx	3 &E
2	(6)	∀x~Fx	4 QE
2	(7)	∀x~Gx	5 QE
2	(8)	~Fa	6 ∀E
2	(9)	~Ga	7 ∀E
10	(10)	Fa ∨ Ga	A [for ∃E on 1]
2,10	(11)	Ga	8,10 ∨E
10	(12)	∃xFx ∨ ∃xGx	9,11 RAA (2)
1	(13)	∃xFx ∨ ∃xGx	1,12 ∃E (10)
	(14)	∃x(Fx ∨ Gx) → (∃xFx ∨ ∃xGx)	13 →I (1)
15	(15)	∃xFx ∨ ∃xGx	A [for →I]
16	(16)	∃xFx	A
17	(17)	Fa	A [for ∃E on 16]
17	(18)	Fa ∨ Ga	17 ∨I
17	(19)	∃x(Fx ∨ Gx)	18 ∃I
16	(20)	∃x(Fx ∨ Gx)	16,19 ∃E (17)
	(21)	∃xFx → ∃x(Fx ∨ Gx)	20 →I (16)
22	(22)	∃xGx	A
23	(23)	Ga	A [for ∃E on 22]
23	(24)	Fa ∨ Ga	23 ∨I
23	(25)	∃x(Fx ∨ Gx)	24 ∃I
22	(26)	∃x(Fx ∨ Gx)	22,25 ∃E (23)
	(27)	∃xGx → ∃x(Fx ∨ Gx)	26 →I (22)
15	(28)	∃x(Fx ∨ Gx)	15,21,27 Sim Dil

	(29)	$\exists xFx \lor \exists xGx \to \exists x(Fx \lor Gx)$	28 $\to$I (15)
	(30)	$\exists x(Fx \lor Gx) \leftrightarrow \exists xFx \lor \exists xGx$	14,29 $\leftrightarrow$I

T46		$\vdash (\exists xFx \to \exists xGx) \to \exists x(Fx \to Gx)$	
1	(1)	$\exists xFx \to \exists xGx$	A [for $\to$I]
2	(2)	$\sim\exists x(Fx \to Gx)$	A [for RAA]
2	(3)	$\forall x\sim(Fx \to Gx)$	2 QE
2	(4)	$\sim(Fa \to Ga)$	3 $\forall$E
2	(5)	$Fa \mathbin{\&} \sim Ga$	4 Neg$\to$
2	(6)	Fa	5 &E
2	(7)	$\exists xFx$	6 $\exists$I
1,2	(8)	$\exists xGx$	1,7 $\to$E
9	(9)	Ga	A [for $\exists$E on 8]
2	(10)	$\sim Ga$	5 &E
9	(11)	$\exists x(Fx \to Gx)$	9,10 RAA (2)
1,2	(12)	$\exists x(Fx \to Gx)$	8,11 $\exists$E (9)
1	(13)	$\exists x(Fx \to Gx)$	2,12 RAA (2)
	(14)	$(\exists xFx \to \exists xGx) \to \exists x(Fx \to Gx)$	13 $\to$I (1)

T59		$\vdash (\forall xFx \leftrightarrow P) \to \exists x(Fx \leftrightarrow P)$	
1	(1)	$\forall xFx \leftrightarrow P$	A
2	(2)	$\sim\exists x(Fx \leftrightarrow P)$	A
2	(3)	$\forall x\sim(Fx \leftrightarrow P)$	2 QE
2	(4)	$\sim(Fa \leftrightarrow P)$	3 $\forall$E
5	(5)	P	A
1,5	(6)	$\forall xFx$	1,5 BP
1,5	(7)	Fa	6 $\forall$E
1	(8)	$P \to Fa$	7 $\to$I (5)
9	(9)	$Fa \to P$	A
1,9	(10)	$Fa \leftrightarrow P$	8,9 $\leftrightarrow$I
1,2	(11)	$\sim(Fa \to P)$	4,10 RAA (9)
1,2	(12)	$Fa \mathbin{\&} \sim P$	11 Neg$\to$
1,2	(13)	Fa	12 &E
1,2	(14)	$\sim P$	12 &E
1,2	(15)	$\forall xFx$	13 $\forall$I
1,2	(16)	P	1,15 BP
1	(17)	$\exists x(Fx \leftrightarrow P)$	14,16 RAA (2)

(18) $(\forall xFx \leftrightarrow P) \rightarrow \exists x(Fx \leftrightarrow P)$ 17 $\rightarrow$I (1)

Exercise 3.4.3

1       $\forall xz(Px \rightarrow Rxz)$
2       $\exists y\forall z(Fy \rightarrow Hyz \& Jz)$
3       $\forall xy(Fxa \rightarrow Gyaa)$
4       $\forall x\exists y(\sim Fx \rightarrow Hy)$
5       $\forall x\exists y\forall z\sim(Fyx \rightarrow \sim Gzx)$

Chapter 4

Exercise 4.1.1

ia	Fa
ib	Fa & Fb
ic	Fa & Fb & Fc
iia	Fa & P
iib	$(Fa \vee Fb) \& P$
iic	$(Fa \vee Fb \vee Fc) \& P$
iiia	$Fa \rightarrow Ga$
iiib	$Fa \& Fb \rightarrow Ga \vee Gb$
iiic	$Fa \& Fb \& Fc \rightarrow Ga \vee Gb \vee Gc$
iva	$(Ga \leftrightarrow P) \vee Ha$
ivb	$((Ga \leftrightarrow P) \& (Gb \leftrightarrow P)) \vee (Ha \& Hb)$
ivc	$((Ga \leftrightarrow P) \& (Gb \leftrightarrow P) \& (Gc \leftrightarrow P)) \vee (Ha \& Hb \& Hc)$
va	$Ha \vee Ga$
vb	$Ha \vee Ga \vee Gb$
vc	$Ha \vee Ga \vee Gb \vee Gc$
via	$Fa \vee Ha$
vib	$Fa \vee Ha \vee Fb \vee Hb$
vic	$Fa \vee Ha \vee Fb \vee Hb \vee Fc \vee Hc$
viia	$Fa \leftrightarrow Fa \& \sim Ha$
viib	$Fa \& Fb \leftrightarrow (Fa \& \sim Ha) \vee (Fb \& \sim Hb)$
viic	$Fa \& Fb \& Fc \leftrightarrow (Fa \& \sim Ha) \vee (Fb \& \sim Hb) \vee (Fc \& \sim Hc)$
viiia	$\sim(Fa \& Ga)$
viiib	$\sim(Fa \& Ga \& Fb \& Gb)$

viiic   ~(Fa & Ga & Fb & Gb & Fc & Gc)
ixa   ~(Fa & ~Ga)
ixb   ~((Fa & ~(Ga & Gb)) & (Fb & ~(Ga & Gb)))
ixc   ~((Fa & ~(Ga & Gb & Gc)) & (Fb & ~(Ga & Gb & Gc)) & (Fc & ~(Ga & Gb & Gc)))
xa   ~(Ga ↔.Ha & ~Fa)
xb   ~(Ga & Gb ↔ (Ha & ~Fa) ∨ (Hb & ~Fb))
xc   ~(Ga & Gb & Gc ↔ (Ha & ~Fa) ∨ (Hb & ~Fb) ∨ (Hc & ~Fc))

Exercise 4.1.2

ia	T	ib	F	ic	T
iia	F	iib	T	iic	F
iiia	F	iiib	T	iiic	T
iva	T	ivb	T	ivc	F
va	F	vb	T	vc	T
via	T	vib	T	vic	T
viia	T	viib	F	viic	T
viiia	T	viiib	T	viiic	T
ixa	F	ixb	T	ixc	F
xa	F	xb	T	xc	F

Exercise 4.2

i   U:{a,b}   F:{a}   G:{ }

        Fa & Fb → Ga & Gb ⊢ (Fa → Ga) & (Fb → Gb)

ii   U:{a,b}   F:{a}   G:{b}

        Fa ∨ Fb → Ga ∨ Gb ⊢ (Fa → Ga) & (Fb → Gb)

iii   Same model as ii

        (Fa ∨ Fb) & (Ga ∨ Gb) ⊢ (Fa & Ga) ∨ (Fb & Gb)

iv   Same model as i

        (Fa ∨ Ga) ∨ (Fb ∨ Gb) ⊢ (Fa & Fb) ∨ (Ga & Gb)

v   Same model as i

           (Fa → Ga) ∨ (Fb → Gb) ⊢ (Fa ∨ Fb) → (Ga ∨ Gb)

vi   U:{a,b}   F:{a,b}   G:{a}

           (Fa → Ga) ∨ (Fb → Gb) ⊢ (Fa & Fb) → (Ga & Gb)

vii   Same model as i

           Fa & Fb ↔ Ga & Gb ⊢ (Fa ↔ Ga) & (Fb ↔ Gb)

viii   Same model as ii

           Fa ∨ Fb ↔ Ga ∨ Gb ⊢ (Fa ↔ Ga) & (Fb ↔ Gb)

ix   U:{a,b}   F:{a}   P is FALSE

           (Fa & Fb) ↔ P ⊢ (Fa ↔ P) & (Fb ↔ P)

x   U:{a,b}   F:{a}   P is TRUE

           (Fa ∨ Fb) ↔ P ⊢ (Fa ↔ P) & (Fb ↔ P)

xi   Same model as ix

           (Fa ↔ P) ∨ (Fb ↔ P) ⊢ (Fa ∨ Fb) ↔ P

xi   Same model as x

           (Fa ↔ P) ∨ (Fb ↔ P) ⊢ (Fa & Fb) ↔ P

xiii   U:{a}   F:{ }   G:{ }   H:{a}

           Fa → Ga, Ga → Ha ⊢ Ha → Fa

xi   U:{a}   F:{ }   G:{ }   H:{ }

           Fa → ~Ha, Ha → ~Ga ⊢ Fa & Ga

xv   U:{a,b}   F:{a}   G:{a,b}   H:{b}

           Fa ∨ Fb ↔ Ga & Gb, ~((Fa → Ha) & (Fb → Hb)) ⊢ Ha ∨ Hb →~Ga ∨ ~Gb

xvi   U:{a}   F:{a}   G:{a}   H:{a}

           Ga ∨ ~Ha, Ga & Fa ⊢ ~Ha

xvii   U:{a}   F:{a}   G:{ }   H:{a}

            Fa & Ga → Ha, Fa & Ha ⊢ Ga

xviii   U:{a,b}   F:{a}   G:{a}   H:{b}

            Fa ∨ Fb, Ga ∨ Gb, Ha ∨ Hb ⊢ (Fa ∨ Ga → Ha) & (Fb ∨ Gb → Hb)

xix   U:{a,b}   F:{a}

            ~(Fa & Fb) ⊢ ~Fa & ~Fb

xx   Same model as i

            (Fa → Ga ∨ Gb) ∨ (Fb → Ga ∨ Gb) ⊢ Fa ∨ Fb → Ga ∨ Gb

Exercise 4.3.1

i   U:{a,b}   F:{⟨a,a⟩}

            Faa ∨ Fbb ⊢ Faa & Fba & Fab & Fbb

ii   U:{a,b}   F:{⟨a,b⟩, ⟨b,a⟩}

            (Faa ∨ Fba) & (Fab ∨ Fbb) ⊢ Faa ∨ Fbb

iii   Same model as ii

            (Faa ∨ Fab) & (Fba ∨ Fbb) ⊢ (Faa & Fab) ∨ (Fba & Fbb)

iv   U:{a}   F:{ }   G:{⟨a,a⟩}

            ~Faa, Gaa → ~Faa ⊢ ~Gaa

v   Same model as iv

            Fa → Gaa ⊢ Fa ∨ ~Gaa

vi   U:{a,b}
            V:{⟨a,a,a⟩, ⟨b,b,b⟩, ⟨a,a,b⟩, ⟨b,b,a⟩}
            ((Vaaa & Vaab) ∨ (Vaba & Vabb)) & ((Vbaa & Vbab) ∨ (Vbba & Vbbb))

            ⊢ ((Vaaa & Vaab) & (Vbaa & Vbab)) ∨ ((Vaba & Vabb) & (Vbba & Vbbb))

vii   U:{a,b}   T:{⟨a,b⟩}

~(Taa & Tab) & ~(Tba & Tbb) ⊢ ~(Taa ∨ Tab) & ~(Tba ∨ Tbb)

viii   U:{a,b,c}   F:{⟨a,b⟩, ⟨b,c⟩,⟨a,a⟩,⟨c,a⟩}

ix   U:{a,b,c}   F:{⟨a,b⟩, ⟨b,c⟩, ⟨c,a⟩}   G:{⟨a,b⟩}

x   U:{a,b}   F:{⟨a,a⟩}   G:{⟨a,b⟩, ⟨b,a⟩}

Exercise 4.4

i   U: $\{m, n\}$ a: m b: m c: n d: n

$m=m, n=n \vdash m=n$

v   U: $\{a, b, c\}$ F: $\{a, b\}$
[((Fa & Fa) & a≠a) ∨ ((Fa & Fb) & a≠b) ∨ ((Fa & Fc) & a≠c)]
  ∨ [((Fb & Fa) & b≠a) ∨ ((Fb & Fb) & b≠b) ∨ ((Fb & Fc) & b≠c)]
  ∨ [((Fc & Fa) & c≠a) ∨ ((Fc & Fb) & c≠b) ∨ ((Fc & Fc) & c≠c)]

⊢ Fa & Fb & Fc

ix   U: $\{a, b,c\}$ F: $\{⟨a, b⟩, ⟨a, c⟩\}$
((Faa ↔ a≠a) & (Fab ↔ a≠b) & (Fac ↔ a≠c))
  ∨ ((Fba ↔ b≠a) & (Fbb ↔ b≠b) (Fbc ↔ b≠c))
  ∨ ((Fca ↔ c≠a) & (Fcb ↔ c≠b) (Fcc ↔ c≠c))

⊢ (Faa & Faa → a=a) & (Faa & Fab → a=b) & (Faa & Fac → a=c)
& (Fab & Faa → b=a) & (Fab & Fab → b=b) & (Fab & Fac → b=c)
& (Fac & Faa → c=a) & (Fac & Fab → c=b) & (Fac & Fac → c=c)
& (Fba & Fba → a=a) & (Fba & Fbb → a=b) & (Fba &Fbc → a=c)
& (Fbb & Fba → b=a) & (Fbb & Fbb → b=b) & (Fbb & Fbc → b=c)
& (Fbc & Fba → c=a) & (Fbc & Fbb → c=b) & (Fbc & Fbc → c=c)
& (Fca & Fca → a=a) & (Fca & Fcb → a=b) & (Fca &Fcc → a=c)
& (Fcb & Fca → b=a) & (Fcb & Fcb → b=b) & (Fbb & Fbc → b=c)
& (Fcc & Fca → c=a) & (Fcc & Fcb → c=b) & (Fbc & Fbc → c=c)

Exercise 4.5.2

i $\forall xyz(Fxy \ \& \ Fyz \rightarrow Fxz), \forall x \exists yFxy \vdash \exists xFxx$
         U: **N**.
         F: $\{\langle m,n \rangle : m<n\}$

         1st premise: T
         2nd premise: T
         Conclusion: F

ii $\forall x \exists y \forall z(Fxy \ \& \ (Fyz \rightarrow Fxz)) \vdash \exists xFxx$
         U: **N**.
         F: $\{\langle m,n \rangle : m<n\}$

         Premise: T.
         ('Every number is less than some other number, and if this other number is
         less than a third number then the first one is also less than the third one.')
         Conclusion: F.
         ('Some number is less than itself.')

iii $\forall x \exists yFxy, \forall xyz(Fxy \ \& \ Fyz \rightarrow Fxz), \forall x{\sim}Fxx$

                  $\vdash \forall xy(Gx \ \& \ {\sim}Gy \rightarrow Fxy \vee Fyx)$
         U: **N**.
         F: $\{\langle m,n \rangle : n \text{ is an even number greater than } m\}$
         G: $\{m : m \text{ is even}\}$

         1st premise: T
         ('For each number there is an even number that is greater.')
         2nd premise: T
         ('If y is an even number greater than x, and z is an even number greater than
         y, then z is an even number greater than x.')
         3rd premise: T
         ('No number is an even number greater than itself.')
         Conclusion: F.
         ('If x is even and y is odd, then either x is an even number greater than y or y
         is an even number greater than x.')

iv $\forall x \exists yz(Fxy\ \&\ Fzx),\ \forall xyz(Fxy\ \&\ Fyz \rightarrow Fxz) \vdash \exists xy(Fxy\ \&\ Fyx)$
            U: **N**.
            F: $\{\langle m,n \rangle$: either m and n are even and m<n, or
                                    m and n are odd and m>n,
                                    or m is odd and n is even.$\}$

v $\forall x{\sim}Fxx,\ \forall x \exists y \forall z(Fxy\ \&\ (Fyz \rightarrow Fxz)) \vdash \forall xyz(Fxy\ \&\ Fyz \rightarrow Fxz)$
            U: **N**
            F: $\{\langle m,n \rangle : \exists k(k{>}0\ \&\ (n=2^{k}(m+1)-1 \text{ or } n=2^{k}(m+1)))\}$

vi $\forall xyz(Gxy\ \&\ Gyz \rightarrow Gxz),\ \forall xy(Gxy \rightarrow {\sim}Gyx),$

                                $\forall x \exists y Gyx,\ \forall x(x{\neq}a \rightarrow Gxa) \vdash \exists y \forall x(x{\neq}y \rightarrow Gyx)$
            U: **N**
            G: $\{\langle m,n \rangle : m > n\ \}$
            a: zero

Index